Discovering Who I Am

Discovering Who I Am is a practical group resource that has been specifically designed for use by clinicians and other professionals within health, education and social care. It supports the running of group sessions for children and adolescents with emotional, social and relationship issues who are learning to better understand and manage their behaviour and emotions.

The resource offers a planning and activity pack for group sessions, uniquely combining four core elements: mindfulness, self-esteem, identity and relaxation. The aim of the group sessions is to improve self-esteem, identity and emotional understanding through simple, experiential and accessible activities.

Key features include:

- a range of activities that can be used as part of a group programme or as stand-alone activities;
- 20 group session outlines which can be adapted for one-to-one sessions;
- photocopiable activity sheets;
- activities suitable for children and young people with a range of abilities;
- resources that are not overly dependent on language.

Packed with easy-to-use session plans and worksheets, this resource will be ideal for educational professionals, clinicians, counsellors and anyone working to support young people with emotional regulation, identity and self-esteem issues.

Geraldine Garwood is an occupational therapist at the South West London and St George's Mental Health NHS Trust.

Joanna Hoskin is a speech and language therapist at the South West London and St George's Mental Health NHS Trust.

Discovering Who I Am

A GROUP RESOURCE FOR CHILDREN AND YOUNG PEOPLE WORKING ON SOCIAL AND EMOTIONAL WELLBEING AND IDENTITY

Geraldine Garwood and Joanna Hoskin

Routledge
Taylor & Francis Group
LONDON AND NEW YORK

First published 2018
by Routledge
2 Park Square, Milton Park, Abingdon, Oxon OX14 4RN

and by Routledge
711 Third Avenue, New York, NY 10017

Routledge is an imprint of the Taylor & Francis Group, an informa business

British Library Cataloguing-in-Publication Data
A catalogue record for this book is available from the British Library

Library of Congress Cataloging-in-Publication Data
Names: Garwood, Geraldine, author. | Hoskin, Joanna, author.
Title: Discovering who I am : a group resource for children and young people working on social and emotional wellbeing and identity / Geraldine Garwood and Joanna Hoskin.
Description: Abingdon, Oxon ; New York, NY : Routledge, 2018. | Includes bibliographical references.
Identifiers: LCCN 2017051811 (print) | LCCN 2018004308 (ebook) | ISBN 9781315172705 (ebook) | ISBN 9781909301917 (pbk) | ISBN 9781315172705 (ebk)
Subjects: LCSH: Group psychotherapy for children.
Classification: LCC RJ505.G7 (ebook) | LCC RJ505.G7 G37 2018 (print) | DDC 618.92/89152–dc23
LC record available at https://lccn.loc.gov/2017051811

ISBN: 978-1-909301-91-7 (pbk)
ISBN: 978-1-315-17270-5 (ebk)

Typeset in Vectora LH
by Apex CoVantage, LLC
Printed and bound in Great Britain by Ashford Colour Press Ltd

MIX
Paper from responsible sources
FSC® C011748

Discovering Who I Am

A resource to support the development of social emotional skills and identity.

A flexible resource designed for children and young people in groups or individually, focusing on social emotional regulation, wellbeing and identity, using experiential activities at different levels with a limited reliance on language.

Geraldine Garwood and Joanna Hoskin
With the Corner House Team

Contents

Acknowledgements

We would like to thank all our colleagues at Corner House for all the work you have put into this project. 'Discovering who I am' was created by all of us and facilitated with the many different young people. We would particularly like to thank Joanna Friedman for her artwork.

We would not have had the breadth of activities without the feedback from the wonderful young people whom we have all had the privilege to work with. Thank you to all of them.

Abbreviations and glossary

1:1	one to one session
CAMHS	Child and Adolescent Mental Health Service
EIF	Early Intervention Foundation
Group members	facilitators and young people
MISER	Mindfulness, identity, self-esteem and relaxation
NICE	National Institute for Clinical Excellence
Talking points	an idea or simple message to reinforce within the course
Topics	the session focus for one week; all topics are related to everyday life
Young people	We use the term 'young people' throughout this book to refer to the participants in the group, whatever their age. Within your setting, you may refer to children, young people, young adults, clients or students. The overall structure of 'Discovering who I am' is suitable for all age groups but activities need to be selected and adapted to meet the age and abilities of each group

Chapter 1

Introduction to 'Discovering who I am'

How it all began. . .

'Discovering who I am' was originally developed as a group resource for a deaf child and adolescent mental health (CAMHS) inpatient unit for 7 to 17 year olds with a variety of mental health and emotional behavioural difficulties. As Deaf CAMHS is a relatively recently developing area, there is not as much research or as many resources available compared to other areas. Therefore, clinicians in this setting regularly create resources. The clinicians wanted to develop a therapeutic group that all the young people could attend despite differences in age, level of ability, difficulties or experience. This would be a group that young people could come to for one session or the whole set of sessions, e.g. a half term, and gain something from attending. However, young people learned the most from attending all of the group sessions. We noticed that the common areas of difficulty that the vast majority of young people were experiencing were in the social emotional skills/wellbeing area: self-esteem, emotional regulation and Deaf identity. It was from these common difficulties that the structure of the group was born: mindfulness, identity, self-esteem and relaxation. Mindfulness and relaxation were used as strategies for coping with emotions i.e. emotional regulation and identity and self-esteem as focuses. Secondary skills or areas that would be focused on through the approach to facilitation included social skills, problem solving, sharing, thinking of others, understanding another person's perspective, how to maintain positive relationships and experiencing these and the general benefits from being in a therapeutic group with others. Additional spaces and groups within the unit focused specifically on other therapeutic areas, but a gap had been identified at the time.

Each group session contains activities in the four elements of mindfulness, identity, self-esteem and relaxation with an everyday topic as a thread linking the activities within the group. A strong focus on experiential activities supports engagement and development of skills and self-esteem. Through the sessions, the young people were given the opportunity to explore and discover who they are; their likes, dislikes, and preferences; their characteristics; and who they want to be etc., all within a supportive nurturing group environment. 'Discovering who I am' was created and topics developed over time with different groups of young people based on their preferences and facilitators' ideas. The activities were also divided into different levels to accommodate different levels of abilities within the same group. Once the resource was 'full', it was felt that others may also find this helpful in different settings.

Many young people in different settings, whether deaf or hearing, could benefit from being in a therapeutic group using the 'Discovering who I am' resource. This could be used in education, health or other settings where young people may struggle, to different extents, with identity, self-esteem and emotional regulation, which can lead to difficulties in relationships, friendships, following instructions, completing work, problem solving, an ability to enjoy activities and feeling good about themselves, building on their resilience. From the quiet ones to the ones who always seem to be in trouble, this resource is for all those young people who may benefit from developing the underlying skills of self-esteem, identity and emotional regulation: skills that have a profound effect on all areas of everyone's life, now and in the future.

Social emotional wellbeing in young people

What is social emotional wellbeing? The National Institute for Clinical Excellence (NICE) advice entitled 'Social and Emotional Wellbeing of Children and Young People' (2013) gives the following definitions for social emotional wellbeing:

- emotional wellbeing – this includes being happy and confident and not anxious or depressed
- psychological wellbeing – this includes the ability to be autonomous, problem-solve, manage emotions, experience empathy, be resilient and attentive
- social wellbeing – good relationships with others and does not have behavioural problems, that is, they are not disruptive, violent or a bully

(NICE, 2013, p. 2).

Social emotional wellbeing has been found to create the "foundations for healthy behaviours and educational attainment. It also helps prevent behavioural problems (including substance misuse) and mental health problems" (NICE, 2013, p. 1).

> *Social and emotional wellbeing provides personal competencies (such as emotional resilience, self-esteem and interpersonal skills) that help to protect against risks relating to social disadvantage, family disruption and other adversity in life. Such competencies provide building blocks for personal development which will enable children and young people to take advantage of life chances. . . .*
>
> *Evidence shows that poor social and emotional wellbeing predicts a range of negative outcomes in adolescence and adulthood.*

(NICE, 2013, p. 2)

One part of the guidance recommends that enhanced self-esteem supports the development of social and emotional skills.

> The emotional wellbeing of children and young people is enhanced through building self-esteem and self-efficacy, reducing bullying behaviour, reducing risk-taking behaviours and supporting the development of social and emotional skills (systematic review of the effectiveness of interventions to promote mental wellbeing in children in primary education). This may also improve all pupils' interest in their learning, lead to better school attendance and improve attainment.
>
> (p. 3)

There is a clear link between the development of self-esteem and social emotional learning as a basis for attainment in life. The foundation of this resource links self-esteem, identity and emotional regulation as the basis for these sessions. If we can enhance and support young people's development of self-esteem as a foundation to their social and emotional wellbeing, evidence shows us that they will have better outcomes in life. "The literature also shows that self-esteem in childhood is important for mental health and physical health in adult life" (Early Intervention Foundation [EIF] 2015, p. 19). The EIF (2015), from their research and extensive literature review titled 'Social emotional skills in childhood and their long term effect on adulthood', describe social emotional learning with five broad groupings:

1 Self-perceptions and self-awareness;

2 Motivation;

3 Self-control and self-regulation;

4 Social skills;

5 Resilience and coping.

These five areas can be a basis for creating goals, are a focus for the approach to facilitation and influence the talking points. Therefore, these can be used within the session as a guide for facilitators to consider when goal setting with young people (see Chapter 3).

- **Why is the group needed?**

Most young people will naturally develop in the areas of self-esteem, identity and emotional regulation in their lives over time. However, for a variety of reasons some young people need more time, extra opportunities or a more focused nurturing approach and a variety of experiences to develop these areas. Some of these young people may have diagnoses e.g. ASD, ADHD, LD, behaviour difficulties, anxiety etc. while others may not. They may be the quiet ones or the loud ones. It is these young people that this resource was created for, to support their growth and development into the teenagers and adults they want to be, achieve and be successful, doing the things they want to do and having positive relationships, feeling good about themselves and building resilience to cope with difficulties in life.

- **How will it help young people?**

Young people will learn about themselves and each other through the activities and the approach of the facilitators and relationships nurtured in the safe space of the group. They will learn with each other and through trying out the things that they have discovered through the activities. They will learn by making mistakes, persevering, being supported and trying again, and experiencing success. By having this shared experience of the therapeutic group with others and sharing their work with the group each week and in the 'event' at the end, it is hoped that they will have the opportunity to develop positive relationships and develop trust in others. Different types of activities expose young people to a range of experiences in a safe environment. The experiential activities include colouring, worksheets, drawing, sticking, games, basic cooking, discussions, sharing, moving around etc.

The group sessions are set up with a nurturing, non-judgemental, understanding, accepting and supportive approach from the facilitators, setting the scene to encourage these positive attributes between the young people as well. All young people are held in positive regard by staff and peers and are allowed to try out skills both in relationships and personally e.g. problem solving and making mistakes, apologising if necessary and trying again. All young people are accepted for who they are and where they are at the time, with the hope of developing skills and improving relationships. Empathy and validation are vital to understanding where young people are coming from and for them to understand what they feel is valid and understandable. This understanding and empathy is also encouraged between the young people. This enables facilitators to work with them from a caring place that tolerates a certain amount of challenge, allowing them to struggle, possibly show unexpected behaviours, try different ways of expressing themselves and be accepted. While tolerating some behaviour, it is vital that natural consequences to challenge behaviour that is not expected is used. This maintains an expectation that young people can develop better ways of coping with emotions resulting in different ways to respond to situations that provoke difficult emotions, and therefore developing more positive relationships now and in the future. The group sessions support young people to become more of the person they choose to be, not what they think is expected of them or what they feel is inevitable. We hope that this resource will give you the ideas and basis to try something new with your young people.

Talking points

There are 20 talking points, which are topics, ideas or simple messages that can be brought up and discussed at opportune moments throughout the group sessions. They are a way of building in important messages to the group without have specific sessions on e.g. emotions, therefore making the sessions more accessible. The talking points can be useful for young people to hear and develop a greater sense of self or of the skills for achieving and being happy in life. Sometimes it might simply be a comment about a young person's performance, something you noticed they have done well, or progress they have made. Others will be longer discussions. They will have their views heard and hear alternative views from others.

Aims of the group session

This resource aims to create the opportunity for young people to discover who they are in relation to what they can do, how they relate to others and managing their emotions. During these sessions, they learn more about themselves and who they want to be, and they continue the journey to become this person they choose through the development of self-esteem, identity and emotional regulation. Experiential learning from doing something and being actively involved is vital to meeting these aims. The aims of the sessions are broken down into four areas:

Discovering and developing a sense of self in relation to own emotions

- To express themselves in a supportive environment.
- To learn how to use mindfulness activities and relaxation in their daily lives to help them feel calmer and overcome difficulties.
- To improve in identifying, coping with and managing their own emotions.

Discovering and developing a sense of self in relation to activities and independence

- To create, work towards and achieve their goals.
- To try new things, make mistakes, possibly fail and try again and succeed with encouragement and support from both the facilitators and other young people.
- To grow in independence with initiating, working on and completing tasks.
- To enhance their own playfulness and sense of fun to support coping.

Discovering and developing a sense of self in relation to others

- To experience positive regard and positive relationships. Experience being accepted non-judgementally for who they are.
- To learn to accept others for who they are without judgement.
- To practise different ways of interacting with others and learn how to get along with others positively.
- To learn about themselves and others and how to see situations from another's perspective.

Discovering who you are

- To decide who they want to be and how they can achieve this.

- To grow in self-esteem and confidence.
- To grow in resilience to difficulties.
- To grow in decision-making, creativity and imagination so young people find things that they enjoy and don't enjoy, therefore discovering more of who they are.

References

Early Intervention Foundation. (2015). Retrieved from www.eif.org.uk//wp-content/uploads/2015/08/Social-and-Emotional-Learning-Final-Report-1.pdf (accessed on 1/08/17).

National Institute for Clinical Excellence Local government briefing [LGB12]. (2013). *Social and emotional wellbeing of children and young people*. Retrieved from www.nice.org.uk/guidance/lgb12/resources/social-and-emotional-wellbeing-for-children-and-young-people-pdf-60521143067845

Chapter 2
The evidence

Chapter Headings

- Introduction
- Mindfulness
- Identity
- Self-esteem
- Relaxation
- Summary

Introduction

This chapter is a summary of the evidence relating to the four elements that the resource focuses on: mindfulness, identity, self-esteem and relaxation.

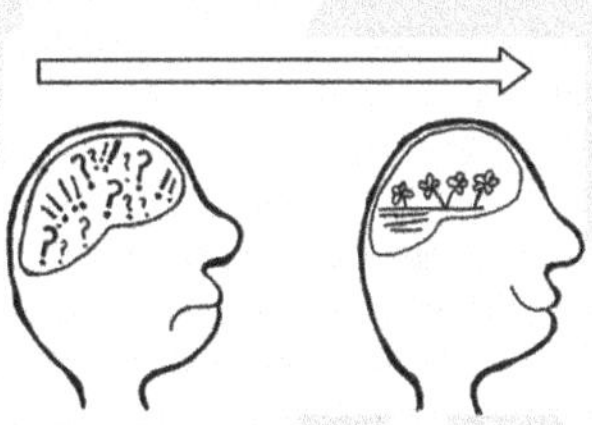

Mindfulness

Identity

Self-esteem

Relaxation

These four elements will be described using the following headings:

1 What is it?

2 How does this develop in young people?

3 What are the benefits for children and young people in their everyday lives?

4 Why is it important for children and young people's development and their futures?

This is a summary of current evidence that we have found useful in facilitating group sessions; it is not a full literature review of the evidence. The current evidence for each of the elements is summarised in order to encourage an understanding the approach to facilitation, the purpose of the activities, why they are important and how they support the development of young people. Knowledge and experience of therapeutic group work, which will be discussed in the next chapter, is as important as understanding the evidence behind the four elements.

Finally, it is also important to consider how each individual benefits from being actively involved in the groups. Their involvement and participation in groups can increase the facilitators' understanding of the individual young people they are working with. When using this resource, consideration must be given to:

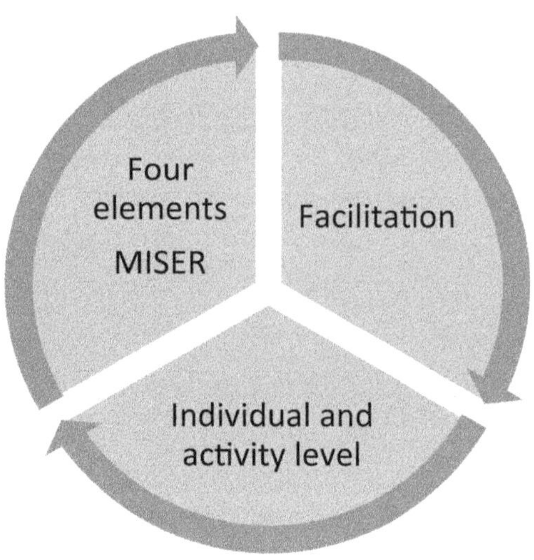

- The individual's experience and skills in the four elements – session activities are suggested in different levels: introduction, developing and experienced.
- The level and type of facilitation techniques that will support an individual within the group – allocation of roles within the group can be shared by adults and young people.
- The individual's strengths and interests – session topics can be selected to meet these needs.

Why Mindfulness, Identity, Self-Esteem, and Relaxation (MISER)?

The National Institute of Clinical Excellence (NICE) provide national guidance, advice and information services for health, public health and social care professionals. In their publication 'What can local authorities achieve by promoting the social and emotional wellbeing of children and young people', NICE, 2013 suggest that social and emotional wellbeing for children and young people is important, and that:

> Social and emotional wellbeing creates the foundations for healthy behaviours and educational attainment. It also helps prevent behavioural problems (including substance misuse) and mental

> health problems. That's why it is important to focus on the social and emotional wellbeing of children and young people.
>
> (NICE, 2013, Introduction, p. 1.)

> Social and emotional wellbeing provides personal competencies (such as emotional resilience, self-esteem and interpersonal skills) that help to protect against risks relating to social disadvantage, family disruption and other adversity in life. Such competencies provide building blocks for personal development which will enable children and young people to take advantage of life chances.
>
> (NICE, 2013, p. 2)

The four elements included in this resource are areas of social emotional learning that have an impact on how well young people are able to manage life's ups and downs as they move into adulthood. The better the young person is able to understand and manage their own emotions and those of others, the better able they are to achieve their goals and overcome disappointments. Both relaxation and mindfulness improve a person's ability to feel calmer and consider their actions when faced with stressful situations and build resilience. Naming and practising these skills within group sessions has enabled individual young people to name and practise them in other settings. So basically if one can feel better about themselves, believing they are a good person and can achieve, and have a better understanding of others and the impact they have on others, the better able they will be to have the headspace to focus on having positive relationships and trying their best at school and in future employment and relationships. These skills can influence outcomes in adult life (Goodman, Joshi, Nasim, & Tyler, 2015).

This resource attempts to give young people a different perspective on others and themselves through positive regard and non-judgemental peer and adult interaction. The sessions provide a safe space to practise being positive towards themselves and others. This is why the co-facilitation of these groups is so important and will be focused on in this resource. Without careful facilitation, the groups are simply a set of activities.

Mindfulness

What is it?

Mindfulness training focuses attention to internal and external experiences in the present moment, without judgement, to enhance young people's attention and focus, and improve memory, self-acceptance, self-management skills, and self-understanding. The NHS Choices (2014) website define mindfulness as giving "attention to the present moment – to your own thoughts and feelings and the world around you" and "knowing directly what is going on inside and outside ourselves, moment by moment."

The mindfulness activities and games included within this resource focus on the senses:

- Touch
- Eating
- Looking at something
- Exploring something through touch
- Moving: walking
- Listening
- Smelling

How does this develop in young people?

Some young people participate in activities that promote focus 'in the moment' such as art, dance, sports, music and martial arts. Many adults seek this focus through yoga and meditation to support their mental and physical wellbeing. Young people develop skills of 'being in the moment' when given opportunities and situations in which they can practise and experience these skills. Young people benefit from having the opportunity to find their 'still, quiet place'. Their skills develop in finding this 'place' and increasing the time for which they can focus (Weare, 2012). Mindfulness is hard to describe, so it is helpful for facilitators to practise mindfulness so that it is fully understood and then they can explain and support the young people more effectively from their experience of it.

What are the benefits for young people in their everyday lives?

Mindfulness has been shown to be helpful because the act of being *present* can be calming, and being an *observer* to one's thoughts and feelings can help objectivity and facilitate change, rather than simply being consumed by thoughts and emotions and acting them out.

So what does this mean for our young people? Mindfulness is about being in the moment, simply being and not caught up in things. This might include being 'caught up' in our own thoughts, worrying about what has happened or what might happen in the future and not being in the here and now. Mindfulness provides more opportunity for making good choices by providing time to think and be calm, then reflect and choose what you want to do, rather than just impulsively reacting. So when difficulties arise, e.g. an argument with a friend, time can be taken to consider actions rather than reacting in a way that was not intended. Therefore, becoming more of the person they want to be (Coholic & Eys, 2016; Ott, 2002; Rempel, 2012; Thompson & Gauntlett-Gilbert, 2008).

Why is it important for children and young people's development and their futures?

Mindfulness activities can provide enjoyment and enable people to find patterns in their thoughts, feelings and behaviour (NHS Choices, 2014). Mindfulness activities can help people notice signs of stress or anxiety earlier and help deal with them better. These skills can support stress management, behaviour control and the development of resilience to stressful situations and events.

The aim of mindfulness activities within this resource is to use them to promote an understanding of self and to have a strategy to support emotional regulation in the sessions, not to teach the practise of mindfulness formerly (Malchiodi, 2014).

Identity

What is it?

Having a sense of one's own identity helps an individual understand who they are. Many aspects of life influence a young people's identity; these include but are not limited to ethnic identity (Phinney, 1990), gender identity (Weinraub et al., 1984), family, friends and community identity (Demo & Hughes, 1990), social class, age, religion, body image (how you think you look to others), internal identity (what you think your personality is), your job and even what fiction books that you read (Kokesh & Sternadori, 2015). In developing this resource, young people's development of a d/Deaf or hearing identity was a key issue, as this can determine communication mode and who they align with socially and culturally (Luey, Glass, & Elliot, 1995 and Holcomb, 1997).

How does this develop in young people?

There are different theories on how identity develops. We have found Erikson's theory (1968) useful in our work. We have found the following four different stages to identity development useful in our work although the children we work with are older. These are:

1 Age 2: The child starts being independent and realises that they are separate beings from their mother or other key carer. When the child is around this age, independence and self-awareness starts.

2 Age 2+: Self-concept starts to develop shortly after self-awareness. Self-concept is the rudimentary definition of self, based on a collection of disconnected traits.

3 Age 3–6: Children begin to make choices and act upon them. Being told that what they chose to do was wrong can lead to shame.

4 Age 7+: The shame that children can feel in the previous stage leads to the child starting to be able to self-evaluate, and at the age of seven, they can take on more accountability for their actions. They learn more about what their culture and social situations deem important and are more involved in peer groups, where they constantly compare themselves to others.

Erikson (1963) suggests that adolescence is the most important period in terms of identity, as adolescents are freer to try out different personalities and roles and can re-evaluate their childhood identity. He called this a "psychosocial moratorium". Erikson (1963) concludes that although friends and family are important for developing an identity, ultimately the individual decides on the identity they create.

What are the benefits for children and young people in their everyday lives?

One of the benefits of having a strong sense of identity is increased self-esteem (Cvencek et al. 2016). Understanding oneself as an individual and in relation to others enables us to identify and make choices in our lives. Erikson (1963) commented that individuals who have a stronger sense of identity are more able to 'adapt and contribute to society'. They know who they are and how they fit and can make decisions or take action to change this as they decide to.

Why is it important for children and young people's development and their futures?

As a person progresses through life stages, many changes in identity occur e.g. child – adult, student – worker. Many theorists also recognise that there is still much refinement, re-evaluation and re-commitment of identity in later life. Many changes in life which may prompt a re-evaluation of one's identity are stressful, e.g. school or job changes, relationship changes such as divorce, changes in health. A strong sense of identity in one aspect of life can be supportive when other aspects of identity are changing.

Within the groups it is important to consider what makes up the individual's own identity and to know the background of each young person in the group – what their family situation and friendship groups are like and how they impact on both their identity and self-esteem. This will enable a validating and empathic approach to each individual, understanding their needs and behaviours etc.

Self-esteem

What is it?

A dictionary definition of self-esteem is 'confidence in yourself and a belief in your qualities and abilities'. Terms associated with self-esteem include pride, dignity and positive self-regard.

Children gradually develop a concept of who they are as an individual, and their view of their worth is dependent on several aspects of their lives, including their physical health and wellbeing, the care and attention offered in their environment, their ability to make and keep friends (Dybina, 2016) and their view of themselves as a 'good' person (Kohlberg & Power, 1981)

It may be useful here to highlight the difference between self-esteem and self-confidence. Confidence comes from the Latin *confido* meaning to trust, and esteem comes from the French *estimer* to value. To have self-esteem is to value and believe in yourself, but confidence is trusting yourself, maybe to do something well or not.

Psychiatrist and philosopher Neel Burton's blog, titled 'Self-Confidence Versus Self-Esteem' (2015), usefully explains this difference between the two and will help facilitators supporting young people in the groups to understand it. He explains that one may be confident in one area of life but not in others, but this does not necessarily mean their self-esteem is high. Naturally, we all probably feel more confident with some things than others. You trust yourself to do well in a maths exam but not to catch score during a basketball game in PE. Confidence is the result of trying and achieving things and having the courage to try in the first place. Therefore, we can give young people the opportunities to experience success within the group setting by offering opportunities to try new things, struggle, maybe fail, learn to tolerate this, try again and succeed. Self-esteem is much more difficult to improve because it comes from valuing yourself rather than looking for recognition or value from others. Within the group, facilitators value each individual for who they are, and this is also encouraged between peers. Things that they do of value can be highlighted to them, which is a step in helping them to value themselves and ultimately to develop self-esteem. Therefore, this resource focuses on a mixture of self-esteem and confidence, but self-esteem is the target for development, with the understanding that it is not a magic resolution.

How does this develop in young people?

Self-esteem is influenced by family, friends, teachers, school activities, social life and society.

- **In infancy**, self-esteem begins when a baby has their basic needs met (e.g. love, nutrition, warmth etc.). When the baby gets the appropriate attention, they are taught that they 'are important, safe and secure'.
- **As a toddler**, this self-esteem is built upon as the toddler learns new skills and becomes more aware of their abilities. They have an increasing awareness of 'self' and their differences from others.
- **At nursery age**, they are more aware of their own emotions and how they can differ from the emotions and feelings of others.
- **In early school years**, they become more aware of their achievements and embarrassments, how they compare to others and whether they meet their own expectations.
- **By eight years old**, children are able to evaluate themselves in many different areas, basing their concept of success on comparison to peers and the messages from peers and adults in their environment.

What are the benefits for children and young people in their everyday lives?

There is obviously a wide variety of benefits for young people from having a strong sense of self-esteem. These include being more likely to feel happier, make and keep friends, try harder when faced with challenges and to take care of themselves physically and emotionally, and less likely to be a victim of bullying.

Leading on from this, Tobia et al. (2017) found links between self-esteem, social exclusion, cognition, emotions and behaviour. If an adolescent has low self-esteem, they will have a greater sense of hopelessness (Karatas & Savi Cakar, 2014) and a higher level of stress symptoms (Kelly, 2004; Schraml et al., 2011).

Why is it important for children and young people's development and their futures?

Self-esteem can provide many protective factors and support mechanisms for managing life's stresses and taking responsibility for one's own actions. Being able to face challenges increases a young person's resilience to disappointments and setbacks. Strong friendships and family relationships provide support when children and young people are vulnerable or experiencing challenges. These support and protection mechanisms can continue into adulthood, as can the skills required to establish and maintain relationships.

Burton (2015) concludes that self-esteem is our thoughts and feelings about our own worth and the basis of reflecting on ourselves, others and the world. People with a healthy self-esteem have more resilience to stresses in life and are more able to take up experiences that will lead to growth and develop meaningful relationships, accepting and forgiving themselves and others. They have more tolerance to take risks and are more able to delight and experience joy.

Relaxation

What is it?

According to the Oxford dictionary, the definition of relaxation is the "state of being free from tension and anxiety". Other words that can be used for being relaxed are to unwind, calm, slow down and let go. So the opposite of relaxation would be tension and anxiety, and the purpose of relaxation would be to release any tension and feel less anxious and therefore calmer.

A few types of relaxation activities can be used. The National Center for Complementary and Integrated Health in the USA states the goal of all relaxation is "to produce the body's natural relaxation response, characterized by slower breathing, lower blood pressure, and a feeling of increased well-being." They describe five types: progressive relaxation, guided imagery, biofeedback/autogenic, deep breathing exercises and self-hypnosis. We have focused on the first four in this resource. We have used a variety of these relaxation types throughout the sessions. For use in this resource, we have divided relaxation into the following:

- **Progressive muscle relaxation**: Muscle groups are tensed and relaxed throughout the body to help the muscles relax and to give the person a sensation of overall relaxation (not recommended for those with heart issues).
- **Guided imagery**: An image or story is described and this is imagined to help relaxation.
- **Visualisation**: Usually visualisation focuses on imagining colour being breathed in and out.
- **Autogenic**: This focuses on different parts of the body and the physical sensations of being warm, heavy and relaxed.
- **Deep breathing exercises**: Focuses on slow, deep even breaths.
- **Sound/music**: Listening to slow, rhythmic music or nature sounds.

They also emphasise the importance of practising relaxation, as with any other skill. The more frequently it is used, the easier it is and the more benefit is felt.

Precautions: Relaxation can make anxiety worse for some people. People experiencing trauma or flashbacks can experience worsening of these symptoms during relaxation. Relaxation can pose a risk to those with heart disease. People with psychosis or schizophrenia should not be involved with any imaginary relaxation, i.e. guided imagery or visualisation.

Note: If you have any concern about doing relaxation activities, please seek advice before using these with young people.

How does this develop in young people?

Opportunities to discuss and experience relaxation can enable young people to use these skills/strategies in other settings. Young people can be taught relaxation skills in age-appropriate activities from an early age: bedtime stories and baths are relaxation routines for very small children. Enabling young people to identify and tell adults when they are tired or don't feel like completing an activity is key to enabling young people to manage their own need for relaxation.

What are the benefits for children and young people in their everyday lives?

When you are relaxed your heart rate declines, your breathing becomes lengthier and deeper, blood pressure decreases or stabilises, your muscles rest and your body can start to repair any damage to it (Lohaus & Klein-heßling, 2000). When people are relaxed they have more time and capacity to think about their next actions.

There have been many reported benefits of relaxation for young people. It can help to reduce general levels of tension and therefore increases feelings of calmness. It provides strategies that young people are able to use when they feel agitated or anxious. This can lead to an improved ability to deal with stress, which in turn may lead to greater resilience. Relaxation has been reported to help to maintain or even develop cognitive functions such as concentration – thoughts slow down and aren't as intrusive or bothering. Self-awareness has also been linked to relaxation. An ability to identify and change how your body feels helps children and young people manage their physical state and level of arousal in some situations (Sternberg, 2001).

Why is it important for children and young people's development and their futures?

The many benefits of relaxation can be important for kids who are struggling. Self-calming strategies support children in managing their level of arousal and can provide an alternative to impulsive behaviours.

Summary

Within this chapter, we have discussed how identity and self-esteem develop and the benefits of learning mindfulness and relaxation for young people. When relaxed, the heart rate and breathing slow and muscles become relaxed, releasing tension. This not only has physical benefits but also promotes a sense of calm and provides time to consider responses in difficult situations, as opposed to reacting impulsively. In practising relaxation and mindfulness activities, young people have strategies to help them feel calmer day to day.

Identity is developed from within ourselves, the environment and our characteristics. Self-esteem develops as we grow from babies to toddlers to children, and through adolescence and adulthood. Low self-esteem can lead to increased stress symptoms. Mindfulness and relaxation can reduce stress symptoms, which is why it is important to offer extra opportunities for learning them within the group. Evidence suggests that both identity and self-esteem can develop throughout life and are not necessarily fixed. Benefits of having stronger self-esteem include improved mental and physical health, continued education and employment, less risk of criminal behaviour and substance misuse, reduced bullying and risk-taking behaviours etc. The evidence summarised in this chapter helps facilitators to empathise with and validate young people's emotions and to understand their situations and what might help. This guides the approach taken by facilitators enabling young people to gain the most from being in the group.

References

Burton, N. (posted 2015). *Self-confidence versus self-esteem*. Retrieved from www.psychologytoday.com/blog/hide-and-seek/201510/self-confidence-versus-self-esteem (accessed on 17/03/17).

Coholic, D., & Eys, M. (2016). Benefits of an arts-based mindfulness group intervention for vulnerable children. *Child Adolescent Social Work Journal*, *33*, 1–13. doi:10.1007/s10560-015-0431-3

Cole, M. B. (2011). *Group dynamics in occupational therapy: The theoretical basis and practice application of group intervention* (4th ed.). New York: SLACK incorporated USA.

Cvencek, D., Greenwald, A. G., & Meltzoff, A. N. (2016). Implicit measures for preschool children confirm self-esteem's role in maintaining a balanced identity. *Journal of Experimental Social Psychology*, *62*, 50.

Demo, D. H., & Hughes, M. (1990). Socialization and racial identity among Black Americans. *Social Psychology Quarterly*, *53*(4), 364–374.

Dybina, O. (2016). Advancing success in behavior and activities as one of conditions for development of self-esteem with children. *European Research Studies*, *19*(2), 251–257.

Erikson, E. H. (1963). *Childhood and society* (2nd ed.). New York: W.W Norton and Company.

Erikson, E. H. (1968). *Identity, youth and crisis*. London: Faber & Faber.

Goodman, A., Joshi, H., Nasim, B., & Tyler, C. (2015). Social and emotional skills in childhood and their long-term effects on adult life. *Early Intervention Foundation*. Retrieved from www.eif.org.uk/wp-content/uploads/2015/03/EIF-Strand-1-Report-FINAL1.pdf (accessed on 30/3/17).

Holcomb, T. K. (1997). Development of deaf bicultural identity. *American Annals of the Deaf*, *142*(2), 89–93. Retrieved from www.ncbi.nlm.nih.gov/pubmed/9154685

Karataş, Z., & Savi Çakar, F. (2014). The university students' life satisfactions: Psychological help- seeking attitude and hopelessness. *Cypriot Journal of Educational Sciences*, *9*(3), 184–193.

Kelly, A. (2004). *Talkabout relationships: Building self-esteem and relationship skills*. Oxon: Speechmark.

Kohlberg, L., & Power, C. (1981). Moral development, religious thinking, and the question of a seventh stage. In K. Lawrence (Eds.), *Essays on moral development Vol. I: Philosophy of moral development*. San Francisco, CA: Harper & Row.

Kokesh, J., & Sternadori, M. (2015). The good, the bad, and the ugly: A qualitative study of how young adult fiction affects identity construction. *Atlantic Journal of Communication*, *23*(3), 139–158.

Lohaus, A., & Klein-heßling, J. (2000). Coping in childhood: A comparative evaluation of different relaxation techniques. *Anxiety, Stress, & Coping*, *13*(2), 187–211. doi:0.1080/10615800008248339

Luey, H. S., Glass, L., & Elliot, H. (1995). Hard-of-hearing or deaf: Issues of ears, language, culture, and identity. *Social Work*, *40*(2), 177–182.

Malchiodi, C. A. (Ed.) (2014). *Creative interventions with traumatized children second edition: Creative arts and play therapy.* In C. A. Malchiodi & D. A. Crenshaw (Eds.). Retrieved from https://ebookcentral.proquest.com 10/8/17

NHS Choices website definition of mindfulness. Retrieved from www.nhs.uk/Conditions/stress-anxiety-depression/Pages/mindfulness.aspx (accessed on 5/14/18).

NICE Guideline. (2013). Retrieved from www.nice.org.uk/advice/lgb12/chapter/What-can-local-authorities-achieve-by-promoting-the-social-and-emotional-wellbeing-of-children-and-young-people (accessed on 12/9/17).

Ott, M. J. (2002). Mindfulness meditation in pediatric clinical practice. *Pediatric Nursing*, *28*(5), 487–490.

Phinney, J., & Appelbaum, M. I. (1990). Ethnic identity in adolescents and adults: Review of research. *Psychological Bulletin*, *108*(3), 499–514.

Rempel, K. D. (2012). Mindfulness for children and youth: A review of the literature with an argument for school-based implementation. *Canadian Journal of Counselling and Psychotherapy*, *46*(3), 201–220.

Schraml, K., Perski, A., Grossi, G., & Simonsson-Sarnecki, M. (2011). Stress symptoms among adolescents: The role of subjective psychosocial conditions, lifestyle, and self-esteem. *Journal of Adolescence*, *34*(5), 987–996.

Sternberg, E. M. (2001). *The balance within: The science connecting health and emotions*. New York: Freeman.

Thompson, M., & Gauntlett-Gilbert, J. (2008). Mindfulness with children and adolescents: Effective clinical application. *Clinical Child Psychology & Psychiatry*, *13*(3), 396–408.

Tobia, V., Riva, P., & Caprin, C. (2017). Who are the children most vulnerable to social exclusion? The moderating role of self-esteem, popularity, and nonverbal intelligence on cognitive performance following social exclusion. *Journal of Abnormal Child Psychology*, *45*(4), 789–801.

Weare, K. (2012). Evidence for the impact of mindfulness on children and young people, 1–12. Retrieved from www.enhancementthemes.ac.uk/docs/documents/impact-of-mindfulness---katherine-weare.pdf (accessed on 5/1/18).

Weinraub, M., Clemens, L. P., Sockloff, A., Ethridge, T., Gracely, E., & Myers, B. (1984).The development of sex role stereotypes in the third year: Relationships to gender labeling, gender identity, sex-types toy preference, and family characteristics. *Child Development*, *55*(4), 1493–1503, doi.10.2307/1130019

Chapter 3

Facilitating groups from preparation to evaluation

Chapter headings

- Introduction
- Planning and preparations
- Running the groups
- Reflections, outcomes and evaluation

Introduction

This chapter focuses on an approach to group facilitation and a way of working in a more therapeutic style with young people; it is not a guide to group facilitation in itself. As stated previously, we assume that facilitators running this group will have experience of group work with young people and therefore some foundation skills. The therapeutic approach to group facilitation is vital for the young people to get the most benefit from these groups. Within this resource, the approach to group facilitation is as important as the activities themselves. The facilitation style attempts to free young people from feeling unable to do things and enable them to achieve the most they can and reach their goals, giving them the skills to deal with difficult situations through the development of self-esteem, identity and emotional regulation.

This chapter is divided into the three stages of facilitation: planning and preparation; running the groups; and reflection, outcomes and evaluating. Each stage requires different skills and focus, which will be described here. The planning stage includes the facilitators preparing themselves, i.e. reading and learning, organising practical issues like space and preparing the young people through meeting them 1:1 to explain the group and manage their expectations. To support the running of groups, the chapter includes tips and ideas for developing a therapeutic style of group facilitation, using tools and strategies and managing difficult situations within the group. The evaluation stage is about making continual adjustments and therefore improving the group through weekly reflections. By using outcome measures and informal discussions for young people and facilitators, both can express their ideas about what they liked and what could have been different.

Keep in mind that facilitation is a skill that needs to be learned by trying it out, much like how we encourage young people to get involved through experiential learning. So get involved with someone who can support you and give it a go. Group work has its challenges, but there should also be moments of joy for both the facilitators and young people.

Note: Throughout this chapter, there are examples of how to explain things to young people. The language we used is written within the examples. These provide suggestions for the language to use but will need adaptation for each child's language understanding, vocabulary, interaction style and expressive language skills.

Planning and preparations

The planning and thought that takes place prior to the group lays the foundation for the whole set of groups from activities, style of facilitation and atmosphere created. Thorough planning, and thinking through any possible obstacles at the beginning, will save time later and provide a more stable and solid group for the young people. If facilitators are calm, containing and managing difficulties with ease within the group, the young people will feel calmer, more open to working towards their goals and able take the risks needed to develop. Therefore, this stage of the process is vital.

Different areas of planning need to be considered, including preparations of facilitators, of practical considerations and of young people. Tasks within the planning stage can be divided between the facilitators, and with good communication this can reduce workload.

Facilitators' preparation

A minimum of two facilitators is required for facilitating each group session so that they can learn from each other, have therapeutic conversations, take on different roles within the same activity, work 1:1 to support young people and manage the group dynamics more effectively. The facilitators will need to have knowledge of the procedures of the setting, knowledge of the young people, a caring and thoughtful approach to working with young people and knowledge of the four elements from the previous chapter: mindfulness, self-esteem, identity and relaxation. These points will be discussed in more detail later in this chapter. More than three adults may be too 'adult heavy', depending on the needs of the young people; however, this may be necessary as some young people may need 1:1 support in the room. Having more adults might support young people's engagement, or it may be decided that they can manage in the group without this to build their confidence and development. If a group member does need 1:1 support, that extra adult needs to be familiar with the content of the session and the ethos and approach taken in the group, which is different from the approach taken in a classroom. The group will be more effective if everyone has a similar approach, otherwise the benefits may be unintentionally undermined and the benefits diluted. To be most beneficial to the young people and the group as a whole, all the adults should be involved in planning before and reflecting after the group and should understand all the individual young people's needs and goals. In some settings, it is useful to have a group of facilitators with two attending the group each week. Whilst we have found rotating facilitators can be helpful, carry-over from one week to the next has been supported by ensuring at least one facilitator attended the previous week's group.

The more **experienced facilitator can then support the learning** of the other facilitator(s) through co-facilitation, not simply being an observer but actively facilitating (we all learn more from 'doing') and reflecting. With two facilitators, there is more time for the facilitators to work individually with young people, which means the facilitators' approach can be adapted to meet the needs of each young person. This is very difficult, if not impossible, to accomplish with only one facilitator.

Young people observe and learn from **therapeutic conversations** between the facilitators, e.g. "The young people seem to be struggling to concentrate, I wonder why?" "Yes, maybe it's because they are finding this activity difficult. How shall we support them to help them focus?" then discussing a way to simplify the activity or try a different activity and come back to that later.

The **talking points** will help facilitators focus on which topics or ideas to highlight in therapeutic conversations or to reiterate within a group. Each talking point has a brief key message which can be used to begin exploration of one topic or idea linked to self-esteem, identity or self-reflection. Talking points' key messages can also be used as a reminder to consider this topic or idea within an activity. Within information for facilitators, the talking points are numbered for ease of reference. This is not in order of importance or development, so facilitators are able to choose the talking points they feel are appropriate for their group.

The facilitators have **different roles** at different times in the groups. One explains and leads the activity and the other focuses on the young people, supporting them to listen and modelling how to complete the activity. This enables the flow to be kept in the group more easily, thus meeting the needs of the group as a whole and the individuals at the same time.

Some young people may have **1:1 time** in the class for a variety of reasons. It needs to be decided with the young people if they want that person in the group or if they feel confident enough to manage the group themselves. Depending on the reason for the 1:1, managing on their own may boost their confidence. However, it may be appropriate to have that extra adult in the group.

Reading and learning

An understanding of the theory of MISER (mindfulness, identity, self-esteem and relaxation) and group facilitation, as well as personal experience using mindfulness and relaxation, is essential for the facilitation of the group.

Basic background reading of MISER can be found in Chapter 2 and should be read by all adults in the group prior to the planning stage. It is important to have an understanding of the benefits of a strong identity and self-esteem for young people in selecting who will benefit from the group and in supporting the development of these areas in the groups. It will also be easier to teach or guide young people through mindfulness and relaxation activities if you have experienced these yourselves and practise them, so practising mindfulness and relaxation regularly is vital to support the growth of others.

Practical preparations

Practical considerations and the setup of the group are discussed here. Facilitators will need to consider:

- **Number of sessions in the set of groups**: The group can be as many sessions as required; it might be a term or a half term. There are 20 topic ideas in this resource for you or the young people to choose from, depending on the number of sessions. The introduction and an evaluation session should be used to start and finish each set of groups.
- **Length of group**: Generally, each group may last an hour or an hour and a half for more experienced young people, if you feel they could focus for this amount of time. There would need to be an active or moving-around element within each group to help the young people to focus.
- **Topics**: Choose the topics that suit your young people, that you have an interest in (as you will be able to be more enthusiastic) and that you have or can get the resources for. If feasible, you could offer a choice to the young people. They could choose the topics in the first session, or a mixture of facilitators' and young people's choices could be best.
- **Talking Points**: Choose the talking points that suit your young people's needs. Your selected talking points will help the facilitators focus on the key messages and ideas that they want the young people to consider throughout the course of group sessions.
- **Location(s)**: The main room should be big enough for a table for everyone to sit around. Some flexibility with the space is helpful, e.g. moving the table out of the way to do some moving-around activities. Some activities need more space for moving or running around, e.g. playground or hall and kitchen facilities are required for some topics. Make sure you have access to the appropriate space for topics prior to choosing them.

- **Equipment**: All the topics include a variety of activities. Many need regular equipment that most services would have, e.g. paper, pens, paint, glue, scissors etc. There are some activities that require other simple equipment, e.g. a blender, bowls, fruit etc. that should be relatively easy to find. For some activities, young people can be encouraged to bring items to the group, e.g. clothes relating to their cultural background, photos for 'My family', items related to their preferred sport or relaxation activity. Giving young people notice to bring things is important. Check that you have all the equipment necessary prior to starting and set up in time for the start of each group.
- **A group folder**: As plans for the group are made, it is useful to keep paper copies of plans and worksheets in one place that is accessible to all facilitators. It may be useful to copy the summary sheets for the topic titles, talking points and activities so this information is available at a glance if the facilitators want to discuss or change anything during reflective review.
- There are two ways of organising facilitation of the set of groups. If there are two facilitators they will do all of the groups. If there are more than two facilitators the timetable including which facilitators will be doing the groups each session should be arranged prior to the start of the groups. We found it helpful to do two weeks in a row to allow for continuity.

Discovering who I am – group planning and evaluation sheet			
Session topics	**Core activities to include**	**How did it go? (include young people and facilitator perspective)**	**Young people + facilitators involved**
DATE **TOPIC** Introduction	M – Clock I – Tell us about you SE – Draw a body R – Breathing		Facilitators A and B
DATE **TOPIC** My body	M – Watch your hand I – My face – what do I look like SE – I like my. . . (describe your body) R – My body when relaxed		Facilitators B and C
DATE **TOPIC** Colour	M – Colouring I – What different colours mean to me SE – Colours I like and why R – Focus on a colour		Facilitators A and c
Staff final evaluation of the group			

Planning activities for the group

Once you have decided on the topics you can think about the activities that will suit the individuals in the group, with the resources that you have available. It is important to consider many areas when planning the groups in order that young people will get the most benefit and avoid potential difficulties. This will also make the group more enjoyable and help facilitators feel organised and confident.

Within each element of MISER are several activity ideas at **different levels**; introductory, developing and experienced. Match the activity level to each individual young person's needs for each element of the group, so different young people may be doing different activities within the same element. If the young people ask why, be honest about it and explain that different people need different things and are working in different ways and that's ok. Anticipate the support they will need for each task. Assign a facilitator to support a specific young person if it is expected to be particularly challenging for them.

It may be helpful to break down the activities in each element into parts to increase the structure and guidance the young people need, especially if they have difficulty following instructions with more than two steps. For example, the identity activity may be divided into two parts, so when one part is finished the second part is explained and carried out. Sometimes a discussion and an activity within an element naturally occur to assist with concentration and focus.

Structure of the group, the space and timings

The actual structure of each group will look something like the following list. Timings have been added along with the initials of the facilitator explaining and leading that particular activity, which should be decided prior to the group. This can be helpful to remind the facilitators what they are doing and leave them freer to focus on engagement and development of individuals.

- Recap from the previous group – 2 minutes – GG
- Introduce topic and go through plan for the group – 2 minutes – JH
- Mindfulness – 10 minutes – GG
- Identity – 17 minutes – JH
- Self-esteem – 17 minutes – GG
- Relaxation – 8 minutes – JH
- Summary – 4 minutes – GG
- Weekly evaluation form (if you decide to complete these)

This may look like a lot and at times it is, so all of these may not be possible, especially if the young people are struggling with listening and engaging etc.; however, all four elements should be included in each group. Therefore, these times are very flexible, depending on how the group is doing. Some parts could take less than a minute – "this is what we're doing today . . ." for the introduction, or for the summary, "this is what we have done today . . ." as the young people leave the room! It may be necessary to make an activity shorter to spend more time on an element or activity that is felt to be more important to those young people. Use this structure to fit your group; however, try to keep all the elements in each group even if some are shorter. Timing is vital for the group to run effectively and the young people to get the most out of it.

Think about how long each activity will take **to maintain timings and flow**. It may take some young people longer than others to complete activities, so for the quick ones have additional activities or ideas at hand or encourage them to complete the activity more thoroughly; they may have rushed and not produced their best work. Roughly plan your times so there is enough time for the last activity, which will also help to keep the flow (see below for more information about flow).

For the session plans, we tried to have a mixture of different types of activities in each group. Obviously, it would not be possible or helpful to plan all of these in each group. However, some of the activities may be used most weeks, e.g. discussions and sharing work and a movement or active activity to help with focus and concentration. Keep in mind which type your group prefers, which helps them concentrate and which is a good challenge. These can keep the groups interesting, offer a diversity of experiences, increase young people's ability to have a go at something new or something that they don't feel they are good at, promote fun and help them maintain concentration and engagement. For example,

- Drama outside games
- Table games
- Games moving around the room
- Creating a story/poem
- Telling a story/poem
- Drawing/colouring
- Craft
- Discussion
- Going around and sharing
- Matching/sorting/sequencing
- Pair work

Use the space creatively and be imaginative. Use the floor, walls and tabletop to create a base for activities. This includes the young people changing position or moving around the room: sitting on the floor for one activity, sitting around the table, standing/moving for something else. Something as simple as this can help them refocus, supporting their concentration. Make sure you have all the equipment that you need for the group. Also make sure you have the right space for activities. All these things should help the young people to engage with activities and each other and stay motivated to try their best, learn and grow.

All staff should be aware of the individual young people's likes, dislikes and triggers, e.g. things that make them angry, anxious or upset. A little about their background and family is worthwhile to know. This information will inform the session's plans and facilitation of groups being sensitive and appropriately addressing relevant areas/topics. If you are working with young people who may need to leave the group during an activity, to either go to the toilet or calm themselves, make sure you have planned where they can go and how they will be supervised if they do need to leave.

Young people's preparation

This section gives ideas about how to choose young people that would benefit from the group, gaining consent from parents/carers and sharing information with other professionals. There is an outline of useful things to include in the 1:1 meeting with each young person prior to the start of the groups. With a variety of young people in the group, it is important to consider and plan how you will meet all their individual needs and the needs of the group as a whole. We have included ideas here about encouraging young people to start to attend the group and helping them know what to expect, especially if they are reluctant at first and need support.

Choosing young people

Choosing young people is important, as this will impact on the atmosphere of the group as a whole and how effective the group of young people can be to each other to support development. Therefore, consider how they will get along with each other and the mix of personalities, e.g. a group of young people who are all louder and dominant might be tricky to manage but may also help them to give each other space and increase their own self-awareness. If this does not seem possible, then consider a different mix of young people. A particular young person might benefit from a different set of peers and be invited to the next set of sessions, if that feels more appropriate.

The young people who might benefit from the group might have difficulties with self-esteem, identity or managing themselves and emotions. These might result in, or look like, a young person having difficulty with making and maintaining relationships, completing work or accessing leisure/play activities etc. As described in the introduction, they may be the quiet or anxious young people who have lower self-esteem and may go unnoticed, as they do not cause any classroom management difficulties. Or they may be the young people who always seem to be in trouble, struggle with class work or play, have lower self-esteem and have difficulty maintaining relationships with both staff and peers. Some young people may have a diagnosis; some may not. The young people may be similar in age or be of different ages. The group was designed to meet a variety of different young people with differing needs, which needs to be managed by the facilitators. Within all these variables, consider how the group will get along with each other and how staff will support and encourage a supportive, accepting and non-judgemental atmosphere that enables each to grow and develop. This is vital to the effective running of the groups.

Informing other adults (parents/carers and teachers etc.)

Parents/carers need to consent to the young people attending the group and older young people may not require parental consent (in line with local policy); however, discussions with family can still be helpful. There is an information leaflet about the group, which can be given to staff and family (consent letter and

'Discovering who I am' leaflet, Appendix 1). Within this leaflet is a consent form requesting any important information that would need to be shared with all facilitators, e.g. medical or behavioural issues/allergies etc. All facilitators should know how to deal with any difficulties arising from these. Carefully follow local policy on these issues.

Meeting young people 1:1

It is important to meet the young people individually prior to the group starting to prepare them for the type of experience they will have. The two main areas to think about are managing expectations and identifying any potential difficulties, and plans need to be created around them. The best time to do this is in the 1:1 pre-group meeting. During the group, it may be relevant to remind young people of the discussions that happened prior to the group, as this can help them accept things they might find challenging. Explaining practical things will also help manage their anxiety of what to expect. This will hopefully address any issues at the start and enable them to therapeutically engage with the group more easily, therefore gaining more from being in the group.

During the 1:1 pre-group meeting, it will be important to include the following points:

- The purpose of the group and general aims (use information sheet in the appendix).
- Who the other young people and facilitators are.
- The ethos of the group (see Chapters 1 and 2 for more details). Staff and young people are encouraged to support each other.
- The four elements of each group: mindfulness, identity, self-esteem and relaxation, and the benefits they can have for young people (see Chapter 2 for theory)
- Different topic each week. In the first group, young people will have the opportunity to choose a topic.
- It's not like being in a lesson.
- Fun!
- Creating and work towards individual goals. Examples and ideas they want to work towards (activity sheet).
- Sharing work will be encouraged after most activities.
- Young people will not be 'forced' to do anything.
- Making decisions will be supported.
- Difficult things will be discussed, e.g. emotions, getting along with others and persevering with challenges. These may be difficult at times but are important skills to work on in the group. Everyone will be supported with these things.

- It is possible to leave the group for a few minutes to calm if necessary, but try to stay in the group and work through the difficulty with others' support.
- Small steps can be taken towards completing difficult activities.
- The activities can be discussed prior to the group to support young people if necessary.
- In some groups, they will have the opportunity to bring in something from home to share with the group. Give examples – clothes, sports kit, photos, examples of their hobbies.
- Discuss that young people will be encouraged and supported to make goals linked to self-esteem, identity and managing emotions etc., which will be reviewed throughout the group and at the end.
- Pre- and post-group evaluation forms can be completed.
- Discuss the 'sharing event' at the end.
- Confidentiality (for young people and staff).

The group is confidential; any information shared within the group should not be shared with others. Therefore, information about other young people should not be talked about outside the group or shared with others. The exception is where there is a risk (use your local policy). Facilitators will only share information if there are concerns about someone's safety or risk. However, it would be helpful to share progress with staff and family if the young people want this. They will be encouraged to share with their families and have the opportunity to do this at the end. Agree what will be shared, and if there are things they don't want to be shared, respect this (if there are no risk issues).

Encouraging thinking, reflecting and problem solving should also be covered in the 1:1. Asking the young people their views and opinions will start to give them a sense of control of difficulties, rather than the difficulties controlling them. They will likely need prompts, suggestions or options.

- Ask the young people what they think will be difficult for them in the group.
- Ask them what they need from others to help them.
- Ask them what they could do themselves to help.

Ask these questions in this order so that the young person is doing as much of the thinking and reflecting as possible. Have a discussion and agree how these difficulties or support needs will be managed. It may not always be appropriate or possible due to the young person's skills. If the difficulty may be between two young people, a discussion should be facilitated supportively to find and agree ways to address these. Therefore, even prior to the group starting, young people are being supported to anticipate difficulties, have these acknowledged and validated non-judgementally and enable calm problem solving. This will give young people an experience of how difficulties will be managed within the group and should reduce any anxiety. Often young people can be made to feel like the problem is them, whereas the behaviour or difficulty may be the problem. By changing the language we use, we can change the perspective of the young people, i.e. not seeing themselves as the problem but seeing the problem outside themselves (externalising the problem). This can include individual difficulties they have, e.g. impulse control and difficulties with specific peers or facilitators who will be in the group.

These talking points may be helpfully used to frame 1:1 pre-group discussions. These can also be brought up where necessary within the groups.

Running the groups

How to create goals with young people

Once young people understand what goals are and have some ideas, ideally they will be able to have their own suggestions for their goals, i.e. the things they want to be better at. Therefore, the goals form can include a list of things they find difficult, and then they can make goals from some or all of these. There are two forms provided, one of which is simpler. Again, use whichever matches the needs of each young person – different forms may be used in the same group. However, if you have your own forms you could use those. Identifying goals can be difficult for many young people, therefore it can be helpful to spark some ideas by asking guiding questions to help explain what goals are.

- What things do you want to be better at?
- Is there anything that you struggle with and wish were easier?
- What things make you unhappy?
- When do you find it difficult? Using the examples they give, you can begin to explore what this means for them, e.g. I always argue with people and don't keep friends, I don't know how to make friends, people never talk to me, I don't want to play on my own at break, I wish they would play with me, I always get into trouble and am told off when it's not my fault etc.
- This can be developed into long- and short-term goals. There is no specific space on the form for this as it won't always be necessary, so it can be added. Remember, the resources can be used flexibly to meet the needs of the young people.
    - Longer-term goal: I will have a friend.
    - Short-term goals:
        - I will make up after an argument with the help of (named person), I will say sorry.
        - I will listen to others' ideas.

- I will politely ask someone to pass me something saying please, wait until they have finished and say thank you.

Only after they have been offered the space to discover their own ideas should suggestions be offered. Give lots of examples. They may be suggestions that you know do not apply to the young people and some that may, so they can say yes and no and create it from their own perspective. Creating goals may not be a very familiar concept or a process they have experienced before. Give young people plenty of time to think about what they want to do. Often they won't be able to think of something straight away. Therefore, start talking about goals when you meet the young person 1:1 about inviting them to the group.

Keep goals positive, e.g. "I will give someone a compliment" and not "I will not be rude". Try to get at least one goal per young person by the second group. Facilitators may have different ideas and areas the young people could benefit from which may not be reflected in the young people's goals. This is ok. Keep in mind your goals for the young people; there will be reasons why they have been invited to the group – e.g. difficulty making friends due to aggressiveness, snatching and not asking nicely – so also focus on these behaviours in the groups. They can also be included with the talking points and can be a useful guide when helping young people think about how they want to improve, but don't push your own agenda. Use the young people's words when making goals so that they 'own' them and will hopefully be invested in them and more motivated to work towards them. Try to make them SMART: specific, measurable, attainable, realistic and timed. The time frame for reviewing or achieving goals may be for a week or by the end of the group or somewhere in between. For example:

- "By the end of the group I will have tried different relaxations and chosen my favourite."
- "By the end of the groups I will present some of my work at the 'event.'"
- "I will go to the group for half an hour this week. Next week I will go to the group for 45 minutes."

The language of the goals needs to match the language skills and knowledge of the young person. The goal devised with the young person might not include a reference to time if their concept of time is limited and they have no language to understand or express this.

Things I find difficult and I want to be better at

- I get angry all the time. I want to stop being angry.
- I want to stop arguing with others. I want to get along better with others.
- I can't ask for help. I want to be able to ask for help when I am stuck.
- I want to make friends. I feel too shy to talk to others.

My Goal	Rating	What can I do to achieve my goal?	What happened? How did it go?	What happened? How did it go?	I'm getting better! (Rating)
By the end of the group I will have tried different relaxations and chosen my favourite.	3 – I'm not very good at relaxing.	Try the different relaxation activities every week.	I did not like the muscle one.	I like relaxing with music.	6
When I start to feel angry I will ask for time out. I want adults to help me make the situation better by talking.	1	Notice when I start to feel angry. Listen to adults when they ask how I'm feeling and answer. Ask for time out when angry. Talk about the situation after.	I got angry and threw my work. I cried. I spoke to adults and felt better.	I felt angry when Jane ignored me. I wanted to hit her. I asked for time out. Adults helped me talk to Jane and it was difficult.	5
I will ask for help once in a group when someone asks me if I don't understand.	2	Be brave. Put my hand up. Tell myself "I can do it". Ask an adult when others are busy.	Ahmed (staff) asked if I had a question, I said no but I didn't understand.	Ahmed (staff) asked if I had a question and I asked a question. It was hard. But no one else was watching.	3
By the end of the groups I will present some of my work at the 'event'.	2				7

Rate 0–10 (0 never, 5 half the time, 10 all the time)

If young people want goals that are not obtainable within the time frame of the set of groups or are out of the scope of the group, e.g. "I want to have two friends and invite them around my house to play", use this as a long-term goal, after making sure this is possible, as other people may need to make these happen (parents/carers). Long-term goals can give a bit more meaning to the group goals, as "I will share my work in a discussion" may not be that motivating, but if it is a step towards a long-term goal of having friends, it may be more exciting and interesting to work towards. Make shorter-term goals that are steps to the long-term goal and that relate to the group, e.g. if a young person is shy and won't talk to others, their short-term goal could be "I will start a conversation in the group" or "I will ask for something that I need, e.g. a ruler".

Short-term goals may be very simple.

- "I will practise different mindfulness activities four times this week."
- "I will complete one activity in the group this week."

Reviewing goals

It is important to review goals to remind the young people of the progress they have made. This will motivate them to work further on their goals and get closer to their long-term goals. This can be done briefly every few groups or every group, whichever is appropriate. The 'My Goals' form has a review column which can be completed to show their progress. The form can be placed in their folder or attached to their paper bodies. At an introductory level, this can include a tick or smiley face sticker; experienced young people could write how they have achieved their goal. The goals may be personal to the young people and they may or may not want to share these at 'the event'.

As stated elsewhere, goals could be reviewed briefly in groups each week or every few weeks and recorded if it is useful. In the last group, progress towards these goals could be recorded on the goals form created at the beginning, as a conclusion to the group and to emphasise their achievements. Rating how well they can do something at the beginning and end can also be a good way to show improvement over time, especially if goals have not been fully met. Goal-based outcomes can be used as a more formal way to evaluate the group's effectiveness. More details about goal-based outcomes can be found at the end of this chapter in the evaluation session.

The sharing 'event'

Prior to the group, plan on the type of sharing event that is possible and most useful for your situation and young people. It could be as big or small as necessary but should be a marked event that the young people work towards. Ideas for sharing work include showing and explaining their work in an assembly, displaying their work on a board in the corridor and having an unveiling. Or it could simply be in the last group sharing with the rest of the group or other people. Each of the young people could invite a friend to come and join the sharing of their work. A bigger event may not be helpful for some groups.

Explain to the young people what the sharing event is and their choices for taking part. Depending on the experience level of the young people, they could also work on organising the 'event' with support, e.g. making flyers, inviting others, organising the time and space etc. This may need to be done outside the group. Don't bring it up often in the groups until the last few groups, as the main focus should be on them discovering themselves, which may be easier if they don't have the potential stress or worry of sharing it with others. The event is simply an addition to support their growth of identity and self-esteem.

Practise with the young people sharing their work with the group prior to the 'event'. Young people should be encouraged to share their own work and enabled to do so with the relevant support; grade their involvement to the level that they are comfortable with. However if things are personal to them, like their goals, they should have the space to choose what to share and what not to. Remember this is a personal learning experience for them. Encourage the young person to identify and address anxieties – they may want and be able to do something even if they are feeling nervous.

Approach to group facilitation

As already mentioned, the skills of the facilitators are as important as the activities themselves in supporting and nurturing the young people in the group. It is important to learn about the theory behind group facilitation, but the only way to really understand it is to do it and get involved. Here, practical applications of group facilitation will be discussed. For the purpose of this resource and the clear explanation of group facilitation, it has been divided into four broad areas: creating a group ethos, using therapeutic tools, managing difficult situations and supporting the group working together (young people and facilitators).

Creating a group ethos

Atmosphere and energy levels

Influencing the atmosphere and energy levels of the group is crucial to the group running well and being effective. Try to get a sense for the group and what the atmosphere is like. If the young people are restless at the beginning, it may be helpful to notice this and comment on it. "You all seem distracted today, what can we do to help us all focus?" Then have an active activity, as this may support their concentration. Remember, it may be worth trying to include something active within each group. Doing something active will often help young people to be calmer afterwards (unless you have young people who become overly excited – you could encourage this person to keep score or something similar). You can bring up the energy levels or focus by being enthusiastic about the activities. Games are great ways to engage young people and can be used as learning tools, as shown in the games throughout this resource. Make the group fun. If the atmosphere is negative, comment on this and try to steer the group into a positive mindset. This may not be possible even with a simple game, sometimes the facilitator has to go with the group's flow and accept that this group will not go exactly to plan. This happens. In the summary, you can remind them of the fun activities and the topic that will be focused on next week. Assure them that feelings come and go and demonstrate your hope that the next group will be different.

Maintaining hope, energy and enthusiasm

It can be tiring when a group is not going to plan. When young people are negative and struggling to engage, this is the time to be understanding, keep hope and maintain *your* energy. This can carry the group and may help the young people to focus. If it doesn't help, keep going! It will be important for their learning that you think they are worthwhile enough to work with, even though they are struggling. Acknowledge their struggles. You could also remind them that you think they are worthwhile and that is why you are trying (in your own words). Remember, they are finding things really difficult at this time and it's not their fault. Peers giving compliments or noting things they are good at can be powerful, so this might be a good time to do a round of compliments and stick them on the paper bodies. Having the young people do something nice for someone else can be easier than for themselves if they are in a negative space.

A positive place with praise

Praise is important for many things, including developing self-esteem, knowing when you are doing something that is expected, and working towards a goal. Young people who are struggling often end up being told what they are doing wrong or to stop doing something and generally being nagged. This can lead to negative thoughts about themselves which impact on their self-esteem; believing they are bad or stupid can make them act that way. So rather than telling them to stop doing something, ask them to do what you expect. Be fun with it. Using humour is a powerful tool. Praise when you see behaviour you expect. Highlight when young people have behaved in a way that works towards or achieves their goal. Be specific with your praise; rather than saying "well done", say what they have done well: "You concentrated and completed that work even though it was difficult, well done." Or linked to a young person's goal to "be a good friend", the praise could be: "You were a good friend there when you gave Sarah the scissors when she asked."

Highlighting and praising young people when they are doing something positive helps them feel good about themselves and know when they have done something they wanted. This reinforces these skills and helps young people understand more clearly what behaviour is expected. Praise whenever anyone makes a tiny improvement, even the smallest thing that is a step towards a goal. Consciously look for these tiny improvements. It is important to keep their goals in mind so that you can comment at every opportunity.

Encouraging peers to support each other

A part of the philosophy of this resource is that young people can support each other, as this not only develops their self-esteem but also their understanding of the impact of their own behaviour on others. You are trying to form a cohesive group amongst the young people where they can learn to trust each other and support each other. Building positive relationships is often tricky for young people with emotional and behavioural issues, so use this as a platform to help them take risks in supportive positive relationships and remind them that this is what the group is about. This doesn't mean that they will be friends after, and that's fine, but they need to be encouraged to get along. This means they need to learn to be kind to each other and not rude or dominating. Giving each other the time and space to engage in conversations about conversations (or interactions) increases young people's self-awareness of their impact on others. It is also a choice that each individual can make to fully engage in the group and not something that can be forced. As facilitators, we offer the space and encouragement, but young people need to accept the challenge and try. This can be made clear to them so they understand what their role is in the group and again what is expected of them and why. Understanding why they have a certain role can help them to be motivated to accept this. The power of the group supporting each individual to work towards their goals should not be underestimated. This is key to an effective group.

Language

The language the facilitators use, e.g. vocabulary, sentence structures, explanations signed or spoken, need to be at an appropriate level for the age and skills of the young people in the group. The participants need to think about the content of the sessions and what it means for them; if the language is too complex, they will not be able to focus on the core skills and knowledge for the four elements. Positive language is vital to support young people learning to be positive about themselves and others.

Using therapeutic tools and strategies

Empathy and validation

Empathy and validation are possibly the most important tools that group facilitators have. Remember, what we're teaching our young people is that all emotions are ok, but it's how we manage them that is important. Many of the young people in the group will have difficulty identifying, understanding, coping with and responding to their emotions in a pro-social way. Through the group, facilitators can try to help young people with this process, and the first steps are empathy and validation. In the group, facilitators may notice an emotional reaction and may comment on it, e.g. I think you look angry now, John, do you know why? (Young person may or may not respond.) Was it because Bill took your pencil? Bill, John feels angry now because you took his pencil, what can we do?

Empathy is 'the ability to understand and share the feelings of another.' (Empathy often gets confused with sympathy, which means 'feelings of pity and sorrow for someone else's misfortune'. Aim for empathy and understanding of the young people, not sympathy for them. Validation is 'recognition or affirmation that a person or their feelings or opinions are valid or worthwhile'. This clearly has links with self-esteem and feeling like the person you are and the skills you have are valid and worthwhile. So it is vital to actively and clearly reinforce this for the young people, which can then support their self-esteem to grow.

These two areas are then a good starting point for trying to understand the group as a whole or an individual in the group who is having difficulty. Also keep in mind their backgrounds and any issues going on for them, which may be as simple as they had an argument at break. Understanding their emotions and why they are feeling that way can in itself lead to a sense of relief that what they are feeling is ok, therefore the start of being able to accept and manage their emotions. It is difficult to write examples in a way that sounds natural, and while you should use your own words that fit with the young people in your group, you may find the example below helpful.

Highlighted here are some tips. Never presume to know what someone else is feeling, as only they know. You're just imagining from your understanding of them and their perspective. Therefore, always check it out with them. Try not to say how you would feel in the situation, as it can be more helpful to imagine how they might feel. Give young people the opportunity to solve difficulties together with the

> A young person starts shouting when a peer takes glue they were using. "Are you feeling angry?" wait for response. If none comes, say "I wonder if that's because Jonny took the glue you were using. I can see how that might make you feel angry." Then say to both of them, "What can we do about this? How can we solve this?" Again wait for a response. You could ask each of them directly to tell you what happened, how it made them feel, empathising and validating these feelings, and encourage them to give each other the space to do so, acknowledging that they will both get the chance. "Let's let Mary finish what she is saying, then we'll listen to you." If they are unable to come up with a solution, one could be suggested. For example, "Mary was using the glue first, maybe you could ask to use it after she is finished?" Wait for a response, and then ask, "Sanjit, would you give the glue after you finish that little bit? Then you could share the glue?"

support, understanding and non-judgemental approach of facilitators. It can feel unnatural to use these strategies at first, but with practice and seeing how the young people respond and grow, it will become easier. Use debriefing after groups to help facilitators reflect on their approach. Approaches for managing difficulties are at the end of the chapter and include supporting young people in resolving disagreements or difficulties.

Facilitating discussions thoughtfully

Discussions are a common activity used in group work and can be very difficult for some young people to engage in. They are used because of their many benefits in developing social and emotional skills. They can last a minute to 20 minutes or more, depending on the needs of the group. Remember that active participation is vital to this group, and it is likely that the type of young people in these groups will struggle with discussion. Therefore, discussions have deliberately been kept short in this resource. Always make sure that all young people are invited to answer a question or share their view, remembering who has and has not spoken. The quiet ones may require a direct question to them and some support. Some will speak up automatically when the group is asked, so be careful that they do not dominate the discussion. Make sure you give space for the whole group, which means there will be silences as young people think or build up the courage to answer. Don't feel that you have to fill the silence with talking; be comfortable with silence. Never force a young person to share. Invite them to answer, but also give them the option to pass. Respect their wishes and move on.

Some may give short answers and need support to give more detail. The following questions may be helpful to ask when encouraging young people to give more details about their stories. This can show interest in their stories and that what they have to say is worthwhile. It may take young people some time to relax, be able to express themselves in more detail and realise that they are interesting and that the group are interested in what they have to say. These questions help to show that the group is listening to them and encourage the group to listen to others. The word 'that' has been used in these examples to represent the topic the young person is talking about and can be substituted for whatever the topic is. These ideas are based on narrative therapy approaches (Vetere & Dowling, 2005).

- **When**: "When did you learn that? When did that start? When did you discover you liked/are good at that?"
- **Where**: "Where did you learn that? Where were you when you first discovered that? Where did this belief/value/characteristic come from?"
- **Who**: "Who taught you that? Who did you see do that? Is there anyone who would be surprised to hear you talk about this? Who did you do that with? Who would value that? Who supports you?"
- More detail: "That's an interesting story/memory/skill. Can you tell us more about that/give us more details, like. . . ?"
- "You were interrupted there. Please carry on, we're interested in what you were saying about that."
- Explain the parts of the story that you particularly liked and encourage other young people to do this too.

> *This quote from Zimmerman and Beaudoin (2002) might be useful:*
> *New meanings [can come for individuals] from noticing and having different experiences, from the raising of questions about these experiences, and from invitations to reflect on [his] choices. This is a very different process from being told directly or in so many words which 'behaviours' were good or bad. It is much more convincing and significant to realise one's own preferences than to be told which ones are 'best'.*

In their work, Zimmerman and Beaudoin identified that

> the key elements of the new developments [for an individual] were what these changes meant: 1) about [the individual] as a person (his identity), 2) about the kind of individual he preferred to be (values, preferences etc.), and 3) about people's experience of him.
>
> (p. 40)

Modelling (including sharing work)

Modelling, in this context, involves the facilitators or even other young people behaving in a way that shows or models an example of the pro-social behaviour that is expected and desired. So modelling reinforces, with your actions, the development that is hoped for the young people. The young people will need to be shown skills, so they can then learn and carry them out, i.e. copy them. This may take much repetition. Therefore, the facilitator's role is to be a model of the skills through the way they behave and interact with the young people and with each other. The young people can see and learn that they can be with others to have their needs met and maintain healthy, mutually beneficial relationships. Remember to notice when young people are doing what is expected and try to 'catch' all of them working towards their goals as often as possible. This reinforces that what they have just done is expected and is a step towards their goal.

Here are some examples of behaviour that can be modelled. Again, use the ones that suit the needs of the young people in the group.

- Making mistakes
- Dealing with a difficult situation
- Resolving an argument
- Coping with emotions with positive emotions returning
- Being in positive relationships with others
- Having fun
- Sharing
- Asking politely for something
- Waiting and being patient
- Teamwork
- Turn taking
- Letting someone else go before you or letting them get their own way over what you want (without being a pushover)
- Winning and losing with grace and kindness
- Listening
- Being assertive and not passive or aggressive
- Finding something difficult and persevering until you achieve it

Many things can be helpful to think about when using modelling. Be natural. Use language that the young people will understand. Actively resolve a difficult situation in the group, i.e. show your problem solving. Show the solution or how something has been overcome. Explain the solution as you go, e.g. "Oh, I made a mistake there and feel a bit embarrassed. Let's use this instead, I think it will work better." Explain the emotions. If you feel embarrassed, say so. Simply explain how things are resolved and the subsequent emotions. "Oh, that made me feel embarrassed but now it's all sorted and I feel better." If it is appropriate and you feel able, make a joke of it. It can be useful to laugh at your own mistakes. Don't make a big deal of it and then move on. Discuss this further if the young people ask or are curious. If they make fun of you, discuss how that makes you feel and challenge them about why they are doing this. It is not a pro-social skill to make someone feel small or embarrassed, and it will not make them real friends. It is important to challenge positively and help them understand the impact of their words on others.

If there is a misunderstanding amongst the facilitators, that's ok. Use this as a chance to model problem solving and positive relationships. Tell the group that you've had a misunderstanding, find a solution together and explain the solution to the group. Fess up, don't cover up! Be honest.

Supporting young people to complete activities

Sometimes young people need help to complete activities. There is a balance between doing something for them and enabling them to do the thinking and the work. Remember the 'work' is not writing something down but doing the thinking that goes behind it. It is ok to do the writing for a young person if they have been able to express their view. Focus on enabling them to do the work for themselves. If drawing or video recording works better than writing for your group, use these different recording methods. Remember that self-esteem develops as we do things for ourselves. We realise that we have the skills and abilities to do things and are a worthwhile person. By doing something for them, what is the message you are sending? Letting young people struggle and experience difficult emotions; explaining, showing and guiding rather than doing for them and grading the activities are all useful ways to support young people to complete activities.

Offering help is all about timing. It can be difficult to know when to step in and when to let the young people struggle. It is difficult to watch someone struggle but essential. Knowing the young people and their level of ability and frustration tolerance will help facilitators with what to say, when not to say anything, when to help and when to let them struggle, overcome and achieve. Being alongside someone as they try can be all that is needed, as is telling them that they are trying really hard even though it looks difficult. It is vital that young people experience attempting tasks and struggling, possibly failing, learning to persevere without their emotions becoming unbearable and then succeeding. Therefore, set up activities so that they will eventually succeed. But supporting the young people to stay with these difficult emotions by encouraging perseverance can be difficult. The facilitator's crucial role is to support young people through the process of experiencing these feelings, naming them, experiencing them and realising they can manage them. They learn to manage these emotions and find ways to carry on despite them and then experience success. Going through this in a supportive, safe environment is essential. A short break from the activity or room may be beneficial. If encouraged, the young people in the group can act as a support too. Remember, feelings don't last forever, they come and go.

The facilitator can ask if a young person is struggling and offer help; "Do you want some help?" This help should be in the form of explaining the tasks again to make sure they understand, then showing them how to do part of it on your own work or sheet, not the young person's, and then they can have another go. It may be necessary to show them an easier way of doing it or simplifying the task. Often young people can approach a task in a way that makes it more difficult. You can say,

"Maybe if you do it this way it might be easier. Have a go. What do you think?" A facilitator could offer to write answers as long as the young person has done the thinking and expressed their ideas. Remember, this is not a class. The focus is on developing their social and emotional learning skills, not educational skills.

Grading activities involves gradually increasing the amount the young people do towards completing a task. This happens over time. Therefore, if the task is to complete a worksheet in the first group, the facilitator may do all the writing, then the next week the facilitator does some and then the young person does a little. Gradually, each week the young person does more. This can also be used with behaviour change. For example, if a young person is struggling to attend the group, they could attend for 20 minutes and then gradually increase this time.

Remember, your impulse as a caring adult is to stop young people from having these difficult emotions by doing tasks for them. You must actively resist this. Young people need to experience difficult emotions in order to learn how to manage them – we learn by doing. The facilitator's role is to support them with empathy and validation. This takes conscious focus and practice and may be an additional skill to those already held by experienced facilitators. Reflection and peer support is vital to the development and continual use of this skill.

If the facilitator has tried to enable the young people to do the activity themselves and it is not working, as a last resort the facilitator could do some bits of the activity: "I'll do this bit, then you can do that bit, ok?" Forward chaining involves the young people starting the task and the facilitator finishing it. The preferred way is backward chaining, in which the facilitator starts the task and the young people finish it. Using grading, the young people would then do more stages of the task until they complete all of it.

Removing barriers to exploration

It is important to try to remove any barriers that will stop young people from taking the risk to try things and developing their skills and confidence. In everyday life, it may not be possible to do this, but within the group we need to nurture the young people and make exceptions for them. This does not mean accepting behaviour that is hurtful to themselves or others; this should be challenged gently and worked with. It does mean that if a young person cannot tolerate one hour in a group, giving them breaks would be appropriate. Or if a young person struggles with a particular type of activity, e.g. writing, they don't have to write in the group – a facilitator could write or they could draw their answers. The group is not about education, it is about the young people developing their social emotional learning skills, which should remain the priority. This may take a shift of focus for the facilitators. However, over the set of groups it may be felt that the young people can tolerate a little more of these difficulties. So, in a graded way exposure to these barriers or struggles could be increased, but this is not necessary especially if they don't want to. They first need to feel that they are understood and are able to develop at their own pace.

Managing difficult situations

When working with young people with emotional and behavioural difficulties, which often have an impact on self-esteem and identity, there will be difficult situations to manage within the group. Otherwise, the young people would not need to attend this kind of group. It is vital to be prepared to facilitate the group in such a way that supports the group as a whole and the individuals within the group. This can be a difficult balance to achieve. Below are some possible difficulties that might arise and ideas of how to navigate the group through them, using them as learning for the whole group. This can be personally challenging for the facilitators, so be prepared to be understanding, patient and flexible. Remember that everyone's safety is the most important thing. It can be exasperating when you have spent time organising a group and think it will be really useful and the group do not engage at all. Persevere and try again next week, acknowledging the difficulties from the previous week. If it were easy, our young people would not need us! Difficult situations that might occur could be refusal to attend, refusal to engage, arguments among peers, aggression towards peers or facilitators, young people walking out, their shouting at facilitators, the whole group being distracted and refusing to fully communicate with facilitators etc. The list is endless! Ways to tackle some of these difficulties and some general strategies are described here.

Everyone's safety is always paramount and should be considered when planning, facilitating and evaluating groups. Here are a few tips, but not an exhaustive list, of ways to manage safety. You may have other considerations, as all settings and young people are different, so always follow local policy and procedures.

- Follow any safety policies and procedures in your workplace; especially know how to get help from others if the need arises.
- Be prepared for the unexpected, hope for the best and remain calm.
- Consider food and other allergies.
- Consider any medical or behavioural issues.
- Risk assess young people, space, equipment and activities.
- Consider how young people will relate and if there are any risk issues that might arise.
- Agree with your co-facilitator on how you will deal with issues. Having a plan can help some facilitators remain calm.
- Get help from staff outside the group.
- Ask the young people to leave if necessary.
- Know where to get support quickly.
- Stop the group as a last resort if needed.

Sensitively respond to whatever is happening in the group. Always consider the reason behind the young person's actions or emotional outbursts – why they are doing it? Knowing their background is vital. This will help you support the young person and react in a calm, positive, nurturing way that offers them the time they need to return to a calm state while challenging any behaviour that is not acceptable or expected. Be sensitive to their needs, be positive and use positive language, and be prepared to be flexible. This might be anything from shortening an activity to completely abandoning all your ideas and doing something different, according to the needs of the group at that time. Try to bring the group back to the plan when the group settles. Another useful point is to avoid power struggles. No one wins. Acknowledge their point of view. If someone does not want to be involved, they can choose not to. It really is up to the young person to decide to engage in the group and choose to learn from it. If they are forced, it won't help them make positive choices or learn from the group, they might just feel resentful.

Young people may refuse to attend the group or engage in an activity for a variety of reasons. Encourage young people to attend or engage in the group but do not force or coerce them. Try to find out what the reason is, and then you can offer various solutions that fit the reason. It will guide the response and support offered. Addressing the cause is more effective. There are many reasons that a young person may be reluctant to attend the group or engage in an activity, e.g. nervous/anxious, worries about looking silly among peers, worries about not knowing what to say, not feeling it will be helpful, just having a bad day, thinking about other things, difficulty concentrating because of other issues etc. If they can't express it, offer them reasons – they may be able to select from your suggestions.

If their reluctance or refusal is about their ability or lack of confidence, encouragement and reassurance will be vital and should be related to the specific thing they are concerned about. Reassure young people that staff are there to manage any individual and group difficulties; therefore, they don't have the responsibility of managing it. If the reason is about other group members, you could offer to have a discussion with both young people and the other facilitator to discuss and try to sort out any issues. It may be worth speaking to both of them individually first to help them empathise and think about compromise and negotiation. Do not force them but use lots of encouragement and negotiation as far as you feel able with that particular young person – this will be in an individual way to match the young person. Explain the activities at the start of the group to give them confidence that they can do it and know what to expect. Reassure them that they don't have to do anything they do not want to. Explain how the group will benefit them and what they will get out of it, reminding them of their goals. They could participate for the first activity. They can leave the group to calm and come back in. They don't know what it will be like unless they try, so tell them they can try it but then they don't have to come back if they've given it a good go. Highlight the skills they have with evidence of what you have seen them do before. Continuing with a group activity if a young person is refusing to engage is a powerful way to encourage them to join in. If the activity is fun, it is hard not to be drawn into it. As facilitator, don't make a big deal of their change of mind. Above all, be enthusiastic about how fun it will be. Tell them what games will be played.

Discussion between facilitators can be useful for the group and for facilitators in deciding how to deal with difficulties, as discussed above. Commenting on the group and how they are getting on can highlight this for them. Young people will often then talk to you about what you've said. For example, if the group are not listening, you could say to the other facilitator, "The group isn't listening today. I wonder why? What do you think?" "Maybe they have . . ." the other facilitator could then pose a possible reason why. A young person may protest at your reason and give you their reason, thereby opening up a discussion and helping them engage where the young people were closed to this before. Go with this discussion until a solution is found. However, remember to keep general talking between facilitators to a minimum again unless it's helpful to the group. All planning should be done prior to the group, so the facilitators should not need to talk about the structure of the group unless it changes due to the young people. It is then appropriate to talk about resolving that issue.

Discussion between facilitators could be used when there are disagreements between young people. To address these, encourage and facilitate a discussion between the young people involved. Talking through difficulties and resolving them is vital but can be very difficult. It may be a new experience to be taken seriously and supported to problem solve within a relationship. Listen to both points of view and try to understand each of them. Remember every emotion and position is understandable, difficult for that person and absolutely valid. Avoid blame or fault; it is not helpful. Acknowledge each young person's responsibilities for themselves and towards each other – disagreements are rarely caused by one person. Then focus on resolving the issue, which is likely to be done by both young people giving a little and meeting at some middle ground. Try to find a solution that is acceptable to everyone and values each individual. Support the young people to think of a solution, but if they cannot, it will then be necessary to make suggestions. If this doesn't work, acknowledge this and move on, remember your responsibility to the group as a whole and to individuals. Get back to the group activities as soon as possible. Carry on the discussion after the group if it is not resolved and tell the young people in advance that this will happen. It may take several weeks to work up to this, as some young people will have difficulty with 'saving face' so experiencing this positively in the group is vital.

Sometimes nothing helps. It's ok to have a group that doesn't go so well and you feel like nothing is achieved. This might even be many groups. Sometimes there may a brief few moments when you have their concentration. If this is the case, do your best to carry on. Using empathy, acknowledge with the group that they seem to be having difficulties and are not engaging, then stop and change activities. Validate this if you can by saying something like "Maybe you're tired as it is last thing in the day" or "Maybe this activity is really difficult, let's try something else." This way you are respecting their difficulties and are more likely to gain their trust, rather than teaching them that they cannot focus and get out of the work. This can be achieved through explaining to the young people that there are some difficulties and you're not sure what's going on. If nothing is working, be honest and comment on this. Ask them what will help. Completely change your plans if the plan is not working. A game is a great way to reengage a group. This is a last resort, as it's important to do what you say you're going to do and to be consistent. Try to carry on for the full length of the group so they know that you will carry on despite their difficulties. This can be containing.

Supporting the group to work together (young people and facilitators)

The whole group working together can be beneficial for many reasons. It encourages teamwork, leadership skills, social skills, building relationship and improvement in development towards goals. The facilitators completing work and sharing it can be useful for supporting the group to work together.

At the end of many of the activities, sharing the work that the young people have done with the group is encouraged. It is often helpful if the facilitators do the activity too, if none of the young people need support and are quietly completing work. They can then share their work or share their experiences during a discussion. However, the work completed and things shared should always be useful to the young people. Sometimes it may not be appropriate or necessary for facilitators to share. However, it can be important for facilitators to share their experience during the mindfulness and relaxation activities, which can prompt the young people to think of their own ideas. Make sure that what you are sharing is helpful for the group. If it will not be helpful, do not share it. Think before sharing.

Things that are helpful when sharing include staying positive and using simple examples. Try to use examples that are ordinary and don't focus on being the best. Focus on your experience of taking part, e.g. taking part in a sports tournament rather than something like coming first or winning a gold medal. Modelling taking part and describing enjoying something may help young people be proud of themselves for even the tiny achievements or enjoyments. Being happy with yourself and your achievements, however small, is a life skill which is being nurtured here. Don't underestimate the importance of the things you share.

The young people should be encouraged to not only work as a team but also take a leadership role. Giving all the young people the opportunity to experience a leadership role can support their development of self-esteem and identity. This might be explaining an activity/game they have done before and leading it or simply reminding the group what happened the previous week. More experienced young people will be able to take the role of leader or model more easily, but try to encourage all the young people at all levels, making a mental note of who has done this so everyone is given the opportunity to be a leader.

Reflections, outcomes and evaluation

Week by week reflections or debrief

A debrief is 'a meeting that takes place in order to get information about a particular piece of work that has been finished, for example about what was done successfully and what was not'. Having a debrief after each group is important and all adults in the group should attend.

The basic aim of this is to think about how the group went to improve both the next group and individual facilitator's skills. This may be improving support given to young people by the facilitators, facilitators working together, planning or leading an activity and improving facilitator skills. Ideally, the meeting would be with space and time to sit down and think once tidying is finished; if this is not possible, it could happen as the room is tidied. Go through anything that you learned, difficulties and how you managed them, anything you personally found difficult, positive skills used when things went well, positive ways young people responded when confronted with a task or managed their emotions well and therefore skills to use again. Discuss each individual young person and how they managed each activity, interacted with others and took steps towards their goals. Be honest. Decide how to manage things in the future, e.g. in the same way or trying something different. Check that you were supporting the young people in the best way and not doing too much for them. Check that facilitators felt supported by each other.

Weekly outcome measures

To review the group as a whole and for each individual young person, it is important for the young people to complete measures before and after their involvement in the group. For some, it is possible to do this for each session, for others it is only possible at the beginning and end of the course. Sometimes young people refuse or struggle to complete forms even with assistance. If this is the case, it is more important that they be engaged in the group than having more official outcome measures.

Collect outcome measure questionnaires at the start of the set of groups and at the end, preferably in 1:1 sessions. These can be used to compare start and end scores to evaluate change over time. There is also the option of using an evaluation form that is completed after each session, which gives more immediate feedback to make improvements for the coming groups. Then meet the young people 1:1 after the course of groups to review their goals and share their evaluations and improvements. These meetings should support young people to reflect on what they have learned and to see how far they have come in achieving their goals. Qualitative discussion is also useful, asking the young people what they enjoyed, what was difficult, what they learned, what they think could have been better etc. These can be used for supporting the young people with reflecting on and learning from their experience and for the facilitators in making improvements for the next time the group is run.

Evaluation

Evaluation of the sessions will work best if it fits with current practice in the location of the groups.

If there is no standard format in your setting, we would suggest considering the following sources of information:

- UCL and the Anna Freud Centre provide information on evidence-based practice and outcome measurement for health and education professionals: www.ucl.ac.uk/evidence-based-practice-unit/publications/professionals

One of the tools recommended on this website is Goals Based Outcomes: www.ucl.ac.uk/evidence-based-practice-unit/docs/publication_files/Goals_booklet_3rd_ed

- The Child Outcomes Research Consortium (www.corc.uk.net/) also provides information about goals-based outcomes and other tools: www.corc.uk.net/outcome-experience-measures/goal-based-outcomes/
- Session Rating Scales and Outcome Rating Scales have been developed specifically for use with children and young people by Scott Miller. These tools are available for individuals to use: https://scott-d-miller-ph-d.myshopify.com/collections/performance-metrics/products/performance-metrics-licenses-for-the-ors-and-srs
- Therapy Outcome Measures (TOMs) are widely used by different groups of therapists and further detail can be found in Enderby et al. (2006).

These formats provide opportunities to evaluate on a week-by-week and whole course basis.

If these systems for evaluation do not suit your setting, it is important to review and reflect on each session more informally, getting views from facilitators and young people if possible. This helps identify what works well and what needs to be done differently, what young people liked, what was helpful and what was not helpful. Here is an example of one early planning and reflective evaluation sheet we used. A blank copy is included in the resources section.

Example of a group planning and evaluation form

Discovering who I am – group planning and evaluation sheet			
Session topics	**Core activities to include**	**How did it go?**	**Young people + facilitators involved**
DATE HERE **Introduction**	M – draw carefully around each other. I – who am I? name, age etc. SE – what do I like about me? R – explain your experience of relaxation.	Enjoyed drawing round each other but not very mindful – need to explain more next time. All able to give info about selves, not all able to identify something they liked, needed adult support.	NAMES OR INITIALS HERE
DATE HERE **My body**	M – look at my hand. I – what do I look like? SE – what do I like about my body? R – clench and unclench hands – discuss how this feels.		NAMES OR INITIALS HERE
DATE HERE **Food**	M – Maltesers/other chocolate. I – what foods do I like? SE – what can I cook? R – Tense/relax activity. Be celery, be lettuce.	Stick to what we said we'd do, went into place a bit too much, linking identity and geography with different foods.	NAMES OR INITIALS HERE

DATE HERE **Colour**	M – choose favourite colour, colour in shape. I – what do different colours mean to me? SE – My favourite colours and why. R – visualise a calming colour.	Worked well linking colour with emotion – they understood this. Next time increase M and R times.	NAMES OR INITIALS HERE
DATE HERE **Everyday life**	M – watch a clock. I – what do you like doing every day? What would you like to do every day (your future)? SE – what do you do every day that you're good at? R – imagine you are going to sleep (lie down and feel the floor).	M – watching the clock worked well. I – some young people got the concept and were able to complete, others found this more difficult. Therefore, need to make worksheet for younger children. SE – Stars worked well.	NAMES OR INITIALS HERE
DATE HERE **Clothes**	M – choose and think about a piece of fabric. I – what do clothes say about us? SE – Make a hat – that's a good thing about me. R – shut your eyes and think about your clothes.	M – went well. SE – difficult as the focus was on making the hat rather than what it says about me. Therefore could pre-make hats then young people focus on sticking things to it and what that means for them.	NAMES OR INITIALS HERE
Staff final evaluation of the group Staff enjoyed running the group. The topics, which created focus, worked well and the regular structure enabled it to be run by different staff effectively. The paper bodies went well, sticking things each week to them to develop identity and self-esteem over time, reminding young people of the work they had done.			

Conclusion

We hope that readers have found within this chapter some useful tips for preparing to run a set of groups. Some theoretical knowledge and experience of MISER and group facilitation are essential. Identifying the young people for the group will depend on knowledge of these areas and experience of facilitating groups.

This chapter has focused on the practicalities of preparing and facilitating a 'Discovering who I am' group. We hope that facilitators have gained knowledge of how to approach group facilitation and feel empowered to try it. Important aspects of group facilitation have been explained, which are as important as the content of the activities. Careful facilitation enables the young people to grow and develop towards their goals, improve their social emotional understanding, identity and self-esteem as well as gain greater understanding of managing their emotions. The structure of the group, the activity elements and debriefing were explored. The importance of writing and reviewing goals with the young people helps to keep focus on where they are at and what improvements they want to see. This also should increase their motivation to participate. Evaluation of goals and the group is vital for seeing improvements over time in a more structured way, for individuals, the group and facilitators.

References

Enderby, P., John, A., & Petheram, B. (2006). *Therapy outcome measures for rehabilitation professionals: Speech and language therapy, physiotherapy, occupational therapy, rehabilitation nursing, hearing therapists* (2nd ed.). Chichester: Wiley-Blackwell.

Vetere, A., & Dowling, E. (2005). *Narrative therapies with children and their families: A practitioner's guide to concepts and approaches*. London: Routledge.

Zimmerman, J. L., & Beaudoin, M-N. (2002). Cats under the stars: A narrative story. *Child and Adolescent Mental Health*, *7*, 31–40.

Chapter 4
Talking points

What are talking points?

Talking points are ideas or simple messages that can be gently and informally discussed within the group. They are especially helpful at times when the group might be doing a simple task, e.g. cutting or colouring in identity or self-esteem activities. In the development of this resource, they have been found to be useful to the young people in facilitating their development in a non-threatening and supportive way. The talking points are a guide and not an exhaustive list. They are designed to be adapted in both language and approach to the specific group at that time. Identify the talking points that will be important for the group of young people you are working with in planning for the group (see Chapter 3, 'Facilitating groups from preparation to evaluation').

Talking points can be useful for young people to hear in order to develop a greater sense of self or understanding of the skills for achieving and being happy in life. It is a way of building in important messages to the group. Sometimes it might simply be a comment about a young person's performance or something you have noticed they have done well, progress they have made or changes they are thinking about. You can facilitate discussion with young people, enabling them to have their views heard and listened to, alongside hearing possible alternative views of others. Many young people are not able to believe good things about themselves or feel it is important to look after themselves when their self-esteem is low. These young people need to experience these messages or ideas in real-life situations. Showing evidence of their development, for example in persevering with a task or managing a tricky situation, over time should support an increase in their belief in themselves. Keep in mind the different messages that you think would be helpful for individuals to hear and look for natural opportunities to mention or discuss these informally.

The talking points cover a range of ideas from managing feelings to common fears, coping with life events to ideas for dealing with difficulties or simply a useful life message. They are deliberately not used as weekly topics, e.g. on anger or assertiveness, as the resource focuses on everyday topics to make the group more natural and engaging and less intimidating. It is the skill of the facilitators to bring these talking points into the groups in a way that is relevant to the young people. Therefore, they supplement the weekly topics and can be used to focus on the goals of the young people and expand on the elements of mindfulness, identity, self-esteem and relaxation, as well as emotional regulation. Some talking points naturally match some of the weekly topics. Remember to discuss with the young people, when you meet them prior to the group starting, that emotions and difficulties will be discussed in the sessions so they know what to expect.

How to use talking points

Read the talking points before the start of the set of groups. Decide which will be relevant to individuals and/or the whole group and keep these specific ones in mind, then look for natural opportunities to bring them into conversations or during simple activities in the group. Use the talking points that you feel are helpful throughout the groups; it is unlikely that all of them would be used within a course of sessions. A situation or question may arise where it would be appropriate to use a talking point spontaneously, which is why it is important to read them and keep them in mind. The talking points that may be relevant to a particular session have been added at the end of the each session plan as a prompt to help you consider them. This is because some talking points may fit naturally with some activities or topics, e.g. healthy lifestyles with the session on food. You may have identified some talking points as important for the group or particular individuals, and topics can be planned with these talking points in mind. Use them in the way that best suits the way you work and your group. Mindfulness, identity, self-esteem and relaxation have not been added to the lists at the end of the session plans, however, because they could be relevant to any session. It is likely that the talking points will also need to be repeated several times. Throughout the sessions, the skill of the facilitator will be to bring these up when relevant to the group so the young people begin to understand these concepts and the relevance to their lives.

Repetition may be needed for learning and supported with other prompts, e.g. noticing when a young person is demonstrating an idea from a talking point that has been discussed and pointing this out as either positive or matter of fact, depending on the situation. Naturally, out of these talking points discussions about goals or hopes for the future may develop, so take the opportunity to record these as group goals or long-term goals. If the young people are struggling with these discussions, acknowledge that it can be difficult talking about these things. In the 1:1 pre-group meeting, remember to mention that they may find some of the discussions in the group difficult and that's ok – the facilitators are there to support them.

1 Mindfulness
2 Identity
3 Self-esteem
4 Relaxation
5 We aren't all good at everything
6 Managing difficulties in life

7 Not knowing is ok

8 Promoting healthy lifestyles

9 Different people have different needs

10 Our actions and language have an impact on others

11 Making mistakes and trying again

12 Persevering

13 Getting along with others

14 Coping with difficulties

15 Everyone is different and that's ok – learn to love yourself

16 Like vs. good at: You can like something that you are not necessarily great at

17 Managing feelings

18 Assertive, compared with passive and aggressive

19 Working towards your own life goals

20 What I think may not be the whole story

1 Mindfulness

Having quiet time to clear your mind helps you mange when things are busy, your thoughts are too much, or you feel angry and are reacting to these thoughts and feelings. The NHS Choices (2014) define mindfulness as giving "attention to the present moment – to your own thoughts and feelings and the world around you" and "knowing directly what is going on inside and outside ourselves, moment by moment." You might not need to quote the NHS choices document, but it's useful to know a formal definition so that you can describe it more confidently to the young people.

Different people like to have quiet time in different ways. Try different activities and see what you like for yourself. Session plans offer different mindfulness activities for you to try. You could try these in your own time too. Some of them you may like and find helpful; others may not suit you. This is ok. Hold onto the ones you like and practise these. Mindfulness is difficult and takes practice, as do many other things in life, like relaxing, reading, writing or improving at sport. Mindfulness activities can help people notice signs of stress or anxiety earlier and help deal with them better. These skills can support stress management, behaviour control and the development of resilience to stressful situations and events.

Each week after the mindfulness exercises, encourage the young people to reflect on whether they liked a mindfulness activity, which aspects helped them and which didn't. Initially this will be difficult, but as each person gives their examples, the group members learn from each other. Flexibility in selecting the mindfulness activity for each session may be needed if some young people are able to identify their preferences early in the course of sessions.

2 *Identity*

It's ok to be different, but it's also important to find people you have similarities with (e.g. groups/ communities).

Although friends and family are important in providing information and influence for developing an identity, it is ultimately the individual's decisions that are key to the identity that they create. Young people can choose to be who they want to be. They don't have to be the person they feel they are 'expected' to be by friends or family or the person that they feel they should be. They don't have to do things they don't want to, to fit in with peers or family. The importance of being yourself to make yourself happy is vital. However, young people will need to feel that they 'fit in' in at least one aspect of their lives to contribute to their identity, self-esteem and sense of belonging.

Sometimes this might mean they are different from others. Reinforce the point throughout the groups that it is ok to be different from others whilst emphasising that everyone has similarities and differences. This point can be made throughout the group by using the activities and by facilitators highlighting differences and similarities. For example, comment on activities that are enjoyed by some members of the group and disliked by others. This process aims to validate young people's differences without judgement, whilst encouraging young people to reflect on their own beliefs and choices or strengths and difficulties. We aim to give the young people the message that 'You can change yourself, who you are and how you act as you get older and it's not fixed. It's ok to change and strive to be who you want to be'.

Remember, when highlighting similarities and differences, avoid judgemental comparisons, as this is counterproductive to improving self-esteem and can lead to arguments. Encourage young people to be themselves and develop a sense of who they are and who they want to be.

3 *Self-esteem*

A dictionary definition of self-esteem is 'confidence in one's own worth or abilities: self-respect'. It may be helpful to discuss this in a session with a focus on self-esteem.

We all have things we don't like about ourselves or things we know we're not good at. Try to think about why you like you and what you're good at. Accepting compliments and giving them to others can sometimes help us give ourselves compliments, value our own abilities and recognise our own strengths.

4 *Relaxation*

Being relaxed is being free of stress and tension. Describe the body sensations (see below) to the group so they start to think about what it feels like to be relaxed or tense. The benefits of being relaxed include being able to feel more focused, feeling calm and having time to think, not experiencing uncomfortable sensations such as feeling hot or having a racing heart. The group participants may think of other things they feel.

Tension: in muscles and in the body from stress

Anxiety: a feeling of worry, nervousness or unease about something with an uncertain outcome (Oxford online dictionary)

Signs of relaxation in your body: slower heart rate, comfortable temperature, relaxed muscles (people in the group may have other examples)

Identify things that help you feel relaxed. These will include things we do every day and will help us to deal with stress and return to feeling calm faster after difficult situations. Exercise helps people feel happy and relaxed.

If anxiety is a particular concern for the young people in the group, this more structured activity could be facilitated. In a discussion, you could informally ask the group to:

- Think of times when they felt tension/stress or anxiety (this does not have to be shared)
- Recall what happened in their body and mind (e.g. feel hot, tense, tight fists, breathing rate increase, heart rate increase, thoughts race, thoughts may be negative etc.) – any answer they give is valid. Record these on the board/paper with discussion and increase explanation from facilitators.
- Remember what they did to feel relaxed and calm after a difficult situation to help them feel calm again. Remember all emotions come and go. Highlight the strategies used, e.g. deep breathing, counting to 10, positive self-talk etc.
- Repeat this exercise to note what happens in their body when they are calm
- Highlight the differences in the relaxed and tense or stressed experiences

Another way to share these definitions could be informally as required, e.g. if a young people is feeling anxious, these feelings and sensations could be discussed in the moment, if appropriate. Other young people could be encouraged to share times when they have overcome feeling anxious and therefore facilitate peer support, acceptance, trust and relationships. This will be especially helpful for any young people who struggle with managing their emotions and become anxious or angry. The discussions will help with noticing and then recognising emotions, helping the young people cope with having these strong emotions and speed up their dissipation.

As with mindfulness, different people find different types of relaxation helpful. It is important to incorporate as many different types of relaxation as possible, offering a chance to develop a preference and practise these. Emphasise that relaxation needs to be practised just like any other skill; it is learned over time. Relaxation does not come easily to some people, but it becomes easier with practice. That's ok.

5 *We aren't all good at everything*

Everyone is good at some things and struggles with other things. This is natural and normal, and we all have different skills and interests. Encourage the young people to identify and recognise their own strengths and struggles, as well as listening to others in the group as they express theirs. The ability of the facilitators to recognise and express their own struggles in an appropriate and containing way will set the tone for sharing information within the group, i.e. share things that will be helpful for the young people to hear.

No one is good at everything, no matter how it appears.

You might think some people are perfect and never have any problems. This is not true.

You don't have to be good at everything.

Even famous people struggle with things. Give examples of celebrities or sports people that the young people will know that have difficulties, e.g. dyslexia etc.

You could also inform young people that in interviews, a question commonly asked is, When something was difficult, how did you overcome it? Educators and employers are looking for good problem-solving skills and people who can be honest.

6 *Managing difficulties in life*

There will always be difficult things that happen in life – events that are stressful, relationship breakdowns, exams, failing essays, being told off etc. The important thing is to be able to find a way to manage the feelings, situations, thoughts and behaviours. It is important in life to talk to people about how you are feeling and find ways to look after yourself, so that you can deal with anything that comes along.

Go around the group and ask the young people to identify something difficult that has happened in the past and how they overcame it. Discuss the feelings (or changing feelings) they had and how they were resolved. Facilitators should have ideas for each individual to prompt them if they cannot think of anything. The facilitator could tell the story for the young person if they agree. Point out the strengths that you think the young person showed when dealing with this experience. Simple events such as being late for school, an argument, forgetting homework, doing an assembly, working with others well or not being picked for a team can be used. The following questions could be used as prompts:

When did it happen?

Where was it?

What did you do?

Who helped?

When did you learn how to do this?

What was helpful?

What was not helpful?

What did you learn?

How were you feeling before and after?

If it happened again, would you do anything differently?

7 Not knowing is ok

It's ok not to know something and ask a question. You don't need to sit there worrying that you don't know how to do something. If you never ask, you will never know.

The young people could be given a challenge to ask something that they don't know in the group. This can be either in a discussion or informally when focusing on a task or reviewing work at the end of the group. After finding something out, the process of asking can be explored. What was it like not knowing something, asking, finding out? How did it feel? What did you think before and after?

8 Promoting healthy lifestyles

Information about promoting healthy lifestyles is increasingly available – the '5-a-day' campaign to increase consumption of fruit and vegetables, the 'change4life' campaign to promote healthy eating and activity. This resource is an opportunity to promote these messages and link to any current local or national campaigns. Consider bringing in the benefits of a healthy diet and exercise throughout the course of groups. Highlight the benefits for the young people in eating well and being active, including:

- Feel happier
- Have fewer physical health problems
- Have improved mental health
- Promotes social interaction and a social network
- Promotes leisure interests

9 Different people have different needs

Different people have different needs, and this means that some people may need things that you don't. This can be seen as unfair! When we think about it, it is fair. We all have different things we are good at and different things we struggle with. Therefore, we need different things to help us achieve and do our best. This talking point may be particularly relevant if group members notice or comment on difference or the facilitators are aware that this may be an issue from previous contact with the young people.

When this talking point is appropriate to the group or a specific activity, go around the group and ask what things they need help with. It is likely that people will say different things, which can be highlighted as an example for this point. Some may need time alone when things get difficult and others may need to talk to someone.

Discuss the difference between a want and a need using examples relevant to the group. One example may be, 'I want to work with a facilitator but I can do the task by myself.' Exploring why the young person wants this in order to understand their motivation can help the young person understand themselves. The young person may not be aware of their own reasons, and these opportunities to discuss will begin the process of self-awareness.

10 Our actions and language have an impact on others

Our actions have an impact on how other people feel. They can make people feel sad or happy, good about themselves or not, frustrated, thoughtful and many other things. Think of different ways you could say the same sentence and make someone else feel good or not, e.g. "Why are you wearing that?" The group could think of other sentences that could be taken in different ways. Role play different ways to say a sentence and the different responses with the facilitators and the group, then have the group think about what each of them were feeling and each of their intentions.

Our actions and language also have an impact on how other people see us. People may think that we don't like them. People may think we are mean and not want to be our friends. People may be scared of us. Depending on how we say things, our facial expression and body language, the opposite to all of these can also happen. If you are thoughtful and kind others may want to be your friend because you make them feel good about themselves and this in turn will help you feel good about yourself.

Our actions and language have an impact on what other people do, e.g. if you take someone's pencil they may shout at you. If you share your ruler, someone may want to play with/spend time with you at break because they think you are nice.

Giving genuine compliments is a way to make others feel good about themselves. Facilitators could ask the group for ways to make others feel good about themselves. Young people may not be used to others being thoughtful and kind, so it might be difficult for them to accept compliments at first; that's totally understandable. But tell them, "Don't worry, it gets easier and we will practise in this group." Several sessions have compliments included, but these could be added to other sessions if useful.

11 Making mistakes and trying again

Explain that everyone makes mistakes and that it's ok to make mistakes. There is always a way to make it better again. This is an important thing to learn, which we have found young people with low self-esteem find difficult. Their view of themselves is often that they can't do things, especially new things. Go around and give examples of when you have made a mistake and how you overcame it. Start with examples from the facilitators and ask young people to contribute when they want to share something. Careful preparation by facilitators is needed when sharing examples to ensure they are appropriate and genuine. Young people are very aware of when facilitators are not genuine.

12 Persevering

It is difficult when you are struggling to do something and this can make you feel lots of different things. It may be anger, sadness, feeling stupid or useless or that you will fail, so what's the point? This can make people feel hopeless and want to give up. But, if you try again and persevere (explain what this means or use other appropriate language – try again, keep at it, repeat) then you will improve and over time succeed.

Find examples from the group of when this has happened for young people. If they are unable to identify anything, think of something you know about them and use that as *a possibility*.

13 Getting along with others

You don't have to like people to get along with them. There will always be people in your class or at work, at your sports or youth group who you don't really like, have arguments with or 'rub each other up the wrong way'. This is ok. Everyone is different and we don't have to like everyone. However, we do need to get on with others, and this is easier if you like them. It's hard to get along with people that you don't really like, but this is a vital skill. So how do you manage getting along with someone if you don't like them?

- If you can, you could avoid them. But this won't help develop the skill.
- Try to understand their point of view. Listen to them. Get to know them better.
- If you get to know them better, you might end up liking them.
- If you have to work with someone, focus on the task, e.g. school project, so that you have a shared goal. Consciously listen to their ideas; it's easy to dismiss someone you don't like. Express your own ideas and ask them to listen if they are not. Remember to listen to them too. Talk to an adult if you're struggling getting on with someone before it becomes an argument or worse. A teacher or group leader may help you both sort out the problem.
- An adult could help you work together until you get used to each other.

Ask the young people for their ideas about how they cope with this. Highlight situations where they have done this before. They may not realise that they have done this.

14 Coping with difficulties

Difficulties happen in life – that's life! Coping at the time is difficult and can be horrible! We learn when we go through hard times and survive.

Be prepared to have a general discussion about this. Even when things are dark and it feels like there is no hope, it will end and there is always something to be learned. Keep going through the hard times and looking after yourself in this, try to do things you enjoy. Often there feels like there is no way out and it's hard to go through this. Talk to someone you trust.

15 Everyone is different and that's ok – learn to love yourself

Set realistic goals and have realistic expectations for yourself. Be happy with who you are now and love yourself and think about the progress you have made, however small. You can always have hopes for the future of who or what you want to be, but also accept yourself as you are now. Both are possible and really important. This links in with trying something that doesn't work out, that's ok, just try again or adjust what you are doing or what you expect from yourself.

16 Like vs. good at: you can like something that you are not necessarily great at

Encourage a discussion around this area. Give examples, e.g. "I like football but I'm not very good. I like playing with people who don't mind that I'm not very good. If it's competitive and people don't pass to me, that's not fun! When people let me join in, I can then get better and they help me. I'm accepted for who I am." Facilitators can think of examples for themselves prior to the group that they are happy to share. They may be simple. "I like doing Sudoku but I can never finish them – but that doesn't matter I still like doing them."

17 Managing feelings

Feelings and emotions come and go and are dependent on ourselves and our surroundings.
Some feelings are nice and others are not; some make you feel more comfortable, some make us uncomfortable. All feelings are ok and natural. Managing emotions is difficult and can have an impact on how we respond and our behaviour. Sometimes feelings can be more intense and more difficult to manage. Sometimes it's difficult to realise that you are experiencing an emotion and you may simply react in a way that you did not intend. Recognising an emotion is the start to being able to manage and cope with them. Then you can decide how to deal with the situation.

Anger, anxiety and sadness are not comfortable feelings. However, they have a purpose. If you're angry, you may fight for a cause, e.g. women campaigning for the vote, or people fighting against racism. Anxiety helps us to manage danger. It's ok to feel any emotion, but it's how you react and learn to deal with it that's important. Feelings come and go. Remember feelings will go away – they won't last forever.

18 Assertive, compared with passive and aggressive

It is hard to get the balance of being assertive and not tipping over into being aggressive or being passive and letting people walk all over you. Explain definitions of these and that they are on a continuum with assertive in the middle and passive and aggressive at either end. What happens when someone is passive? They don't stand up for themselves, they don't say anything and people don't notice them, and they might feel left out and not listened to. A person who comes across as aggressive, even if it is not meant this way, can make others feel scared and not want to be their friend and they might get into trouble. A person who is assertive stands up for what they believe in, is able to express their opinion and feel heard. You could use famous people or those on TV shows to give examples. Each way might or might not get your needs met, but an assertive person is more likely to have a positive outcome and be left feeling ok.

Comments can be made when young people are assertive in the group to demonstrate what it looks and feels like in the moment. Simply talking might not fully support the young people to understand what they mean and how to be assertive, so noticing practical examples will reinforce this message.

19 Working towards your own life goals

Consider what having 'life goals' means. Do you have goals you want to work towards in life? What are they? What will help you achieve in your life? These can be helpful even to guide the choices you make about things, e.g. if you want to be a builder then it might be helpful to study physics and science. If you don't know what you want, that's ok, you can make decisions about the things that you enjoy and things that make you happy. This might naturally lead to being somewhere that makes you happy. Having small goals is as important as having longer-term goals. It is important to have goals that give you purpose now as well as further into the future.

20 What I think may not be the whole story

Remember that our thoughts and perceptions are based on our feelings and this can have an impact on our view. We don't know what someone truly thinks or feels or what their intentions are unless they tell us. Be careful about making assumptions, as you may get it wrong. Wrong assumptions may then impact negatively on how you feel about a person or situation. If you gather more information and consider other possibilities, things might look different.

Chapter 5
Session plans

We have created session plans for 20 sessions and originally ran the group in two blocks of 10 sessions. However, we then carried out the group over a half term, which was fewer sessions. Sometimes the same young people did the group for two half terms and we used different topics. Therefore, this is flexible and the facilitators should decide what is best for their group and setting. The young people can choose the topics. Each session can be delivered as a stand-alone event, as long as an explanation of the four elements is given. We have found, however, that there is far more benefit from all the young people attending all the sessions to grow as a cohesive group and build relationships etc. to be able to trust and take risks with each other. This also means they benefit over time in a cumulative sense.

The topics

1. Introduction
2. My body – what do I look like?
3. Colour
4. Senses: sound, vibration and smell
5. Food – what do I like?
6. Food from around the world
7. Clothes – what do I like?
8. Clothes from around the world
9. Everyday life – what do I like?
10. Sport – what do I like? My teams and games
11. Exercise – my body and relaxation
12. My body – growing and changing

13 Gender – my body and stereotypes

14 Relationships and my family

15 Nature

16 Places

17 Culture

18 My future

19 My perfect place – summary and evaluation 1

20 Preparing for the event – summary and evaluation 2

Choosing topics

It is important to start with the introduction session as this sets the scene for the whole course. Then any topics can be chosen by you and/or the young people in the first session, depending on which the facilitators have the resources for and feel confident and enthusiastic about. There are two summary and evaluation sessions (19 and 20). Both of these or one of them can be used to finalise the set of groups. Like the introduction, it is important to complete at least one of them. It may depend on what type of 'event' you choose to have whether you use one or both of them.

How to facilitate the activities in the four elements

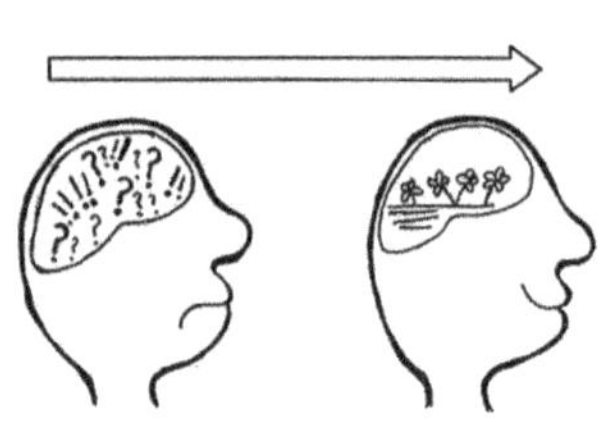

Mindfulness

Identity

Self-esteem

Relaxation

It is useful to have signs, words and ways to explain these areas to the young people, as they can be tricky to explain and understand. Remember, experiencing them is essential, so don't spend long on these. Ask if any of the young people know the four elements (mindfulness, identity, self-esteem, relaxation) or have done activities with them before. They may have ideas of what they are, in which case you could explain the elements using their ideas. They should not all be explained in the first group, as this would take too long. Gradually do it over the first few weeks. Some ideas are listed below, but they need to be adapted for the needs of the young people in each group.

Mindfulness activities

Explanation: "Mindfulness helps you to stay focused and concentrate on school or work. It can help people to deal with anger and other emotions that distract them from being happy. Sometimes other skills become easier when we are mindful. When we're doing mindfulness, we are trying to focus on what is happening in our bodies or around us at that moment. Focusing on the here and now, not the past or future. It's not easy. It is a skill like all others that sometimes needs time to be practised and experienced to understand it. So it may seem like a waste of time at first, but carry on with it. There is lots of research that shows it's helpful for both young people and adults."

The length of time for the mindfulness activities has not been given in the session plans. The aim for young people is 5 minutes. Therefore start small, even just 30 seconds, and work up to 5 minutes or increase the time each week; 5 minutes is not often possible for our young people. Do the mindfulness activities twice with a break in between to reflect and ask young people to say something about their experience. Focus, reflect and share, focus again. This can help get young people into a calmer state, as the first one can be a bit noisy as everyone settles into the group. Let young people know that this is what will happen. Remember, 5 minutes may not be reached, depending on the group you are working with – that's ok. So go with how much your group is managing, but challenge them too.

Ideas to encourage discussion and sharing of experiences:

- What was it like?
- What did you notice?
- Were you able to focus?
- What was distracting you?
- It's ok to be distracted. Remember non-judgementally/gently notice and accept this then refocus. It's not a bad thing. That's the whole point. Mindfulness is a skill that has to be learned. Keep trying.
- How can you focus more next time?

Identity activities

Explanation: "Identity is who you are as an individual. The things that make you special and who you are. It includes your appearance and personal characteristics, things you're good at, likes, dislikes etc. It is also the thing that make a group of people different from others, e.g. supporters of a particular sports team. Having a strong sense of identity helps people understand who they are and helps develop self-esteem. It helps people be flexible and achieve the best they can. Our identity develops as we grow up, and lots of things influence it, like family, friends, school, teachers, community, race, religion, hearing or deaf etc."

The groups start with creating an outline of their bodies. Facilitators keep these safe and bring them out each week. Each week the work from the group will the added to them, either directly on the paper bodies or worksheets cut out and stuck on. If there is limited time, after the group facilitators could cut out their worksheets and the young people quickly stick them on the week after.

Self-esteem activities

Explanation: "Self-esteem is the confidence in who you are and what you can do. It grows and develops throughout life. Having a stronger sense of self-esteem means people feel happier, make and keep friends, and will try harder when faced with challenges. They will also be more likely to take care of themselves physically and emotionally and less likely to be a victim of bullying. Self-esteem helps to manage life's up and downs too when difficult things happen."

Young people are invited to actively complete activities to gain a sense of achievement and belief that they can do things and are worthwhile.

Relaxation activities

Explanation: "If relaxation is the opposite of being tense, then we need to understand this. We are tense when we are highly aroused, e.g. angry, anxious, worried, stressed etc. Our muscles become tense and our breath quickens, we may have more worries etc. So being relaxed means having fewer worries and it means slowing our bodies down, including breathing and letting go of the tension in our muscles and bodies."

These activities are designed to give young people the opportunity to experience different types of relaxation activities and to try them out in a safe environment. Make sure everyone is comfortable. Again use an amount of time that suits your group and try to increase this through the sessions. Let young people know that this is what will happen.

It is hoped that the repetition and routine of the activities will help the young people to focus, as they will know what to expect.

Appendix A and Appendix I contain details of each of the elements. This can be shared with young people.

The levels

As explained in Chapter 2, the activities in each element are divided into levels that are matched to the individual young people's skills. There are three levels, and therefore at least three activities in each element of each group. Different activities can be used sensitively with different young people if beneficial for the group.

- **Introductory** – for young people who have little experience or understanding of the topic or area of focus. These activities may also be suitable for younger group members or those with additional needs.

- **Developing** – for young people who have some experience and understanding of the topic or area of focus.
- **Experienced** – for young people who have participated in similar activities before. They will have experience and understanding of the topic or area of focus.

Practice

Some activities in different weeks are similar, especially the mindfulness and relaxation activities. These can be used as practice, as these are skills that need to be learned through doing them again to find out which ones you prefer. Acknowledge they are similar and that through practising people get better and refine their skills.

Choosing activities

Feel free to use this resource flexibly. Therefore, if particular types of activities work well for your groups, e.g. games, arts and crafts, then use more of these activities. The whole resource has been designed to have a variety of activity types throughout, so feel free to match activity types to your topic and group.

Table of topics, activities and resources

Here is an overview of the activities for all sessions and resources required to help with planning the groups. They can be swapped around and used flexibly and creatively to match the equipment at your setting and the needs of the young people. For example, if some of the young people are deaf, you may not want to use the listening relaxation activities and could use relaxation activities from other topics that would suit your group more.

No.	Topic	Mindfulness	Identity	Self-Esteem	Relaxation	Activity Sheets
1	Introduction	What is mindfulness? Pouring water	Who am I? Draw an outline of your body	What am I good at? What do I like? Picking topics for the groups	Slow breathing	• Group rules • Topics list (table) • Topics list (stars)
2	My body – what do I look like?	Look at your hand	What do I look like? Focus on your face	What do I like about my body? Compliments about the body	Progressive muscle relaxation	• Progressive muscle relaxation scripts (in relaxation section)
3	Colour	Colouring a shape	What do different colours mean to me?	What is my favourite colour and why?	Visualising colours	• Colours and emotions • Colour and my t-shirts/ uniforms
4	Senses: sound, vibration and smell	Sensory object and finger painting	Hate – like – love continuum	What senses do Using our senses to help us relax	Favourite sense to relax OR Relaxation music	• List of preferences • Love, hate, like symbol sheet • Be good to yourself-

5	Food – what do I like?	Eating a Malteser/raisin mindfully	What foods do I like?	What can I cook?	Tension and relaxation (illustrated by spaghetti)	• Food I like plates • I can cook table • Words to describe relaxation and tension
6	Food from around the world	Eating fruit mindfully	What foods do I like from different countries?	Making smoothies	Tension and relaxation (celery vs lettuce)	• Under/on/above ground • Smoothie glass outline
7	Clothes – what do I like?	Fabric – feeling different textures mindfully	What do your clothes say about you?	Make a hat and write words that describe you	How do your clothes feel on your body?	• Activities and clothes • Types of clothes • Characteristics I have now table
8	Clothes from around the world	Describe what others are wearing without looking	Clothes people wear around the world	The clothes I like	Choose a fabric you like and feel it	• Clothes you wear table • Words to help guide relaxation
9	Everyday life – what do I like?	Miming with an everyday object	What do I like doing every day?	What am I good at?	Sleeping activity	• Stars of things I am good at • Things I do every day
10	Sport – what do I like? My teams and games	Complete a maze	Sports personalities	Identifying sports I'm good at and sports I like	Moving in rhythm with your breathing	• Sports skills list • Relaxation table with instructions
11	Exercise – my body and relaxation	Thinking about my muscles	What do I do to help my body relax?	My body is good at. . .	Balance and breathing	• What helps you relax? • Relaxing/not relaxing • Situations to feel tense/ relaxed • How I can relax?
12	My body – growing and changing	Watching a clock	Create your own timeline	What do I like about my body? Favourite age?	Being small and getting bigger	• Timeline sheet • Growing and changing
13	Gender – my body and stereotypes	Focus your mind on a part of your body	What does gender mean to me? Expectations and characteristics of boy/girl Challenging stereotypes	I like being a boy/girl because. . .	Breathing	• Jobs and skills comparison • Identity and gender – positives and challenges
14	Relationships and my family	My favourite person	Who am I for other people? Roles and responsibilities	Who am I? Personal qualities and characteristics	Thinking about your partner's breathing	• My skills and qualities • What am I like?
15	Nature	Mindful nature walk	What animal would I be?	Leading games	Growth	*Pictures and objects to be collected from local resources by facilitators to suit the group*
16	Places	Focus on a point in the room	Map: where do you come from?	Comfortable places vs. uncomfortable places	Progressive muscle relaxation	*Maps to be collected from local resources by facilitators to suit the group* *Photos of local places to be taken by facilitators prior to the session*
17	Culture	Cultural objects	World festivals and faith	Family/school events	Count down	• Things that make me feel good

18	My future	Choice – group decide	Timeline and hopes for the future	My achievements	My future relaxation activity	• My future – I want to be. . .
19	My perfect place – summary and evaluation 1	Choice – group decide	Describing a memory	Creating your perfect place	Favourite individual relaxation activity	• Mindfulness and relaxation activities I like
20	Preparing for the event – summary and evaluation 2	Choice – individual	Discovering who I am	Presenting your work	Favourite group activity	

Talking points

The talking points are ideas or simple messages that can be gently and informally discussed within the group. The title 'Talking Points' has been added into sessions where they might be useful. For some sessions many talking points are added, but it is not suggested that all talking points be discussed in one group. This has been done as a way to help facilitators consider which talking points might be appropriate for their group. Other ones may be important to the young people, so use them where necessary. The full description of talking points and how to use them is in Chapter 4.

Session 1 Introduction

Explain the following within this session.

- **Explain what the group is for**: Include the frequency and time the group takes place. Explain that all young people are there for different reasons and we need to respect and give each other the space they need to develop their skills. Everyone will be working towards different goals.
- **Make some ground rules**: Ask for the young people's ideas for ground rules and write them on a big piece of paper to put up each week to be used as a reminder. Try to write them from a positive perspective, e.g. change 'don't interrupt' to 'give each other time to contribute', but use their language. They might include things like: give each other time to contribute, no mobiles, respect others (but get some specifics), try to understand each other's perspective, try your best, have fun (should always be there), speak one at a time, let others finish speaking before you speak, hands up to speak, respect other people's opinion – it might be different from yours and that's ok, encourage one another, speak nicely to others, ask for help, share, take turns etc. This must include confidentiality to non-risk information (see Chapter 3 for more details). Information about this is included in guidelines for preparing the young people for the group (see 'Meeting young people 1:1') and reinforced during the discussion of group rules in Session 1.
- **Each group will have activities covering the four elements**: Mindfulness, identity, self-esteem and relaxation will be covered using a different topic each week. Sometimes different young people might be doing slightly different activities to suit them. These can be discussed in more detail throughout the sessions.

NOTE: The activities in this session are shorter, as more time will be spent on introducing the group and explaining the elements etc.

Mindfulness

What is mindfulness? Focusing on pouring water

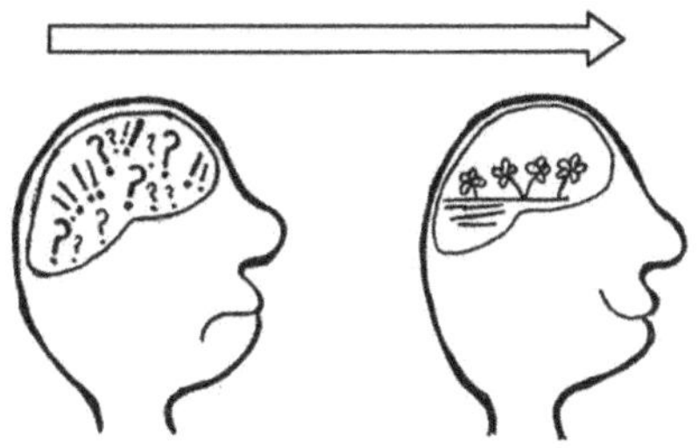

Aim

- To experience and practise being in the moment, focusing on the here and now.

Instructions

- Very briefly describe mindfulness activities using the explanation above if helpful.
- Explain that facilitators will pour water from one jug to another for a decided length of time. Young people will try to focus on this. They will have the opportunity to share their experiences and then the group will try again.

Identity

Who am I? Draw an outline of your body

Me

Aim

- Draw your body outline.

Instructions

- Explain that identity is who we are.
- Give the young people the option of which body they want to create from the following. Explain that each week they can add their work to these to create their identity.

- **Introductory**: On large pieces of paper (that are as tall and wide as the young people), have the young people lay on their paper on the floor. Draw around their bodies (avoiding personal areas). The young people can fill these in after.
- **Developing**: Draw a large body outline on a big piece of paper, e.g. A3/A2, copying an example.
- **Experienced**: Draw their body outline on whatever sized paper they like. This will be more of a self-portrait.
- Remind the group that these do not need to be finished, as they will be added to throughout the groups, e.g. next week they can draw their face.

All: Go around and everyone shares their work by showing it to the group and saying something about it. Remind everyone about group rules (listening to others, confidentiality etc.).

Self-esteem

What am I good at? What do I like? Picking topics for the groups

Aims

- For everyone to identify a skill, talent or like.
- For everyone to tell the group something about themselves.
- Choose topics for the set of groups.

Instructions

- Ask each young person to tell the group something they are good at or that they like about themselves. This will differ in the different levels:
- **Introductory**: Ask young people to share a fact about themselves or something they like, e.g. eye colour, hair colour, football etc.
- **Developing**: Ask young people to share two things about themselves that they like.
- **Experienced**: Ask young people to share something they like about themselves and why that is important to them.
- Draw or write these and add to the paper bodies.

Note: Review any group rules that need to be reinforced; encourage group members to review, reword and follow their rules as often as is needed.

Choosing topics

- Pick topics for the set of groups. A variety of resource ideas is included to help you do this. Use the one that matches your group.
- **Introductory**: Have a small number of topics for the young people to choose from. Use the word and picture for the topics. This may be a choice from two topics each. Have two topics cut out from the list. Each young person could choose one or two topics depending on the number of young people and weeks the group will run for.

- **Developing**: Have more topics that the young people can choose from. Each young person could have one choice.
- **Experienced**: Explain to the young people that you want them to agree amongst themselves what topics they want to have for the rest of the groups. Use all the topics. They have a discussion with each other, facilitated by the adult as little as possible, and negotiate and come to an agreement about which topics they want to do. More explanation can be given in order to help them make a decision, e.g. the activities that would happen in different topics. They may need some guidance about how to do this together, e.g. maybe they all choose two or they rate them and the highest rated topics are used etc.

Relaxation

Slow Breathing

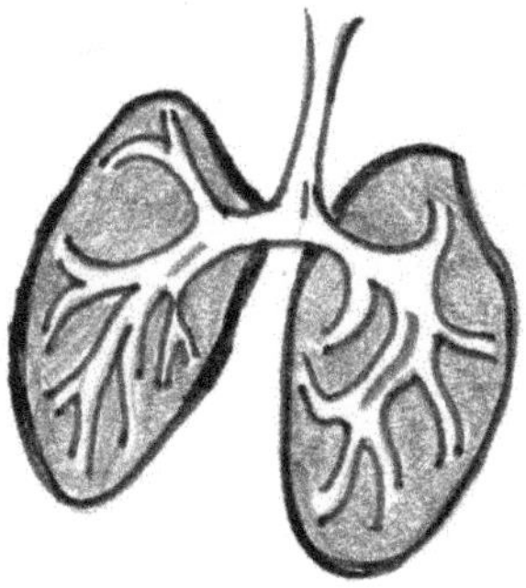

Aim

- To experience and practise relaxation activities to promote calmness and reduced tension.

Instructions

- Simply explain relaxation – Being relaxed means feeling calmer and reducing the tension in our bodies.
- **All**: Invite young people to sit comfortably in their chair. Have them close their eyes if they wish. Tell them to focus on their breathing – in and out – for a period of time. Encourage them to breathe slower in and out if this feels ok to the group. Then discuss how easy or difficult this was or anything they noticed. Simply focusing on and thinking about breathing may be enough of an introduction to relaxation at this point.

Talking Points related to this session

- Different people have different needs.
- We aren't all good at everything.
- Everyone is different and that's ok – learn to love yourself.

Activity sheets for session 1

Group rules

1. Take turns (give information and take information)
2. Confidential – what does this mean?
    a)
    b)
    c)
3.
4.
5.
6.

Topics list (laminate and bring to each session once completed)

My body – what do I look like?	Clothes	Gender – My body and stereotypes
Colour	Clothes from around the World	Relationships
Senses of sound, vibration and smell	Everyday Life	Nature
Food	Sport and Exercise	Places
World Food	Exercise and Relaxation	Culture
My body growing and changing	My Future	Review or Event

Topics in stars

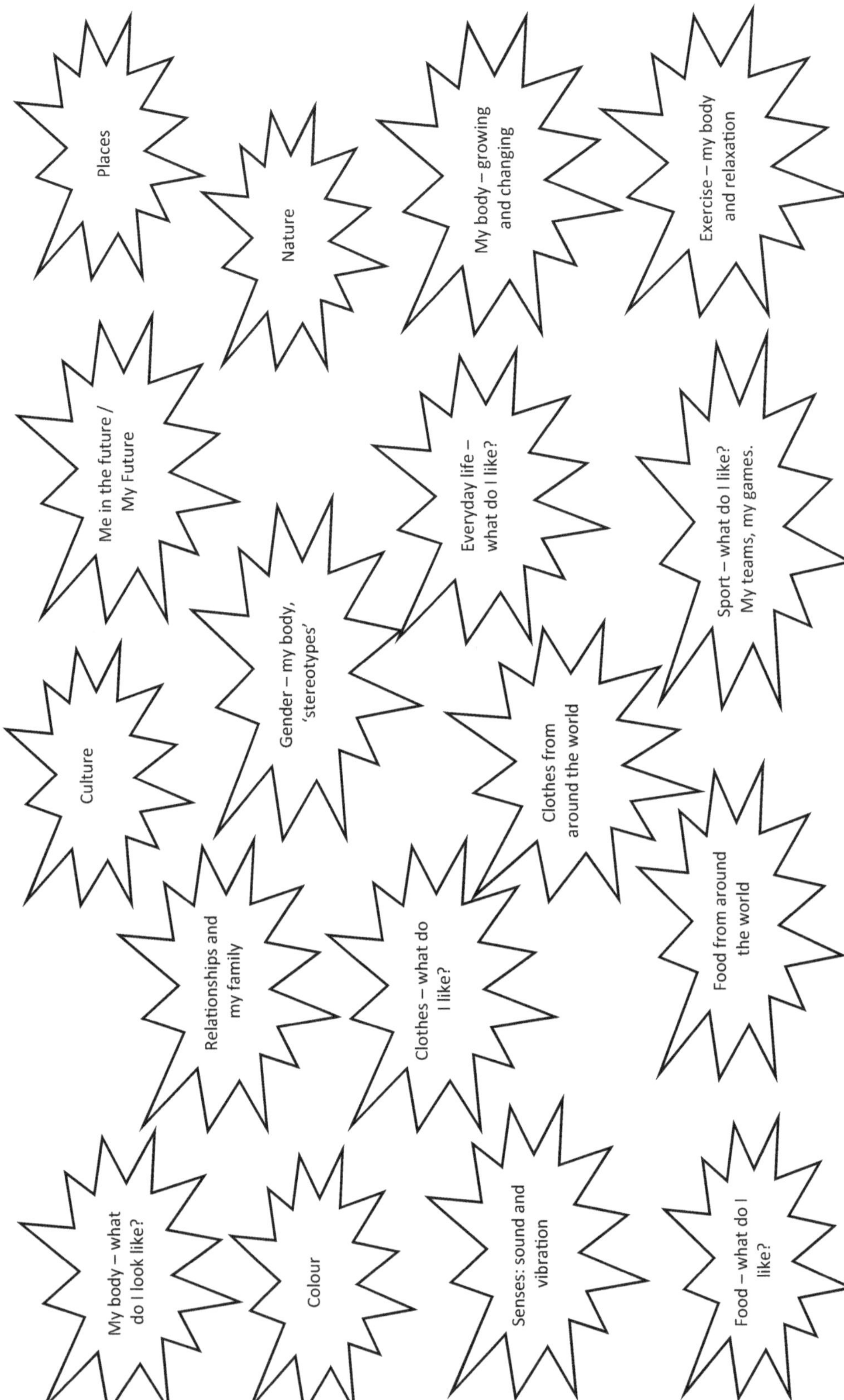

Session 2 My body – what do I look like?

Mindfulness

Look at your hand

Aim

- To experience and practise being in the moment, focusing on the here and now.

Instructions

- Have young people look at their hand for the agreed length of time and try to focus on it.
- Give them the opportunity to share their experiences.
- Then focus again.

You will need

- Something to sit on comfortably.

Identity

What do I look like? Focus on your face. Draw your face on your body.

Aims

- Notice and describe your own physical appearance.
- Notice differences between others and start to think about 'Who Am I?'
- Think about the physical traits you have. What makes you look like you?

Instructions

- **All**: Young people will spend some time drawing their face on their paper bodies. This could include using mirrors to check what they look like. Reminders may need to be offered, e.g. What is the colour of your eyes? What is the colour and style of your hair? What shape is your face? etc. to help them with the detail.

Then:

- **Introductory**: Being directive may help. For example, "Draw eyes, nose, mouth, hair and ears on your paper bodies from the previous week. Use a mirror to notice things about yourself you might not have noticed before."
- **Developing**: Try to encourage the group to notice things about others (in a non-judgemental way), e.g. someone has brown eyes and someone else blue etc.
- **Experienced**: On the board, draw a rough bar graph with number of people up one side and the different eye colours at the bottom. Everyone can put their eye colour on the bar graph (with help if necessary). This is a visual representation of their variety and how they fit in with others. This could also be done with arm span or height etc.

Equipment

- Worksheet to record height, eye colour and other body features
- Pencils/pens
- Outlines of bodies
- Tape measure to measure height
- Mirrors to draw a self-portrait

Self-esteem 1

What do I like about my body?

Aim

- To point out parts of the body that may or may not be liked (and why).

Instructions

- **Introductory**: Have them name body parts and point to their body parts they like the most.
- **Developing**: Have them draw on the body outline what they like the most. Can they think what they like about it?
- **Experienced**: Have them draw/write on the body outline what they like the most and why.
- Consider what other people may like about their body/face.
- How can you emphasise the parts of your body you like to increase your confidence? For example, wearing the colour green makes my green eyes stand out more.
- Discuss what is more important to you in a friend – their looks or their character? (Emphasise the importance of character compared to looks.)
- Draw or write on the arrows parts of your body that you like. You could also write a reason why you like it. This could include a piece of clothing/sense of style. For example, I like my hands because I can draw with them or sign; I like my feet because I can play football; or I like my green eyes.

Equipment

- Outlines of body
- Pencils/pens
- Big arrows

Self-esteem 2

Compliments about the body

Aims

- To learn what a compliment is.
- To think about how to pay compliments.
- To practise paying compliments about each other.
- To practise receiving a compliment.
- To consider body language.

Instructions

- Try to focus on compliments for physical appearance.
- **Introductory**: Ask them to say or draw something nice that they like about the person on their right.
- **Developing**: Think about and discuss what compliments mean and how to say them to someone else. Give a compliment to the person on your right.
- **Experienced**: Discuss what compliments mean and how to say them to someone else about something specific, e.g. nice eyes or nice hair. What is it like to receive a compliment? How does it feel? How do you react to a compliment? How would you like to react to a compliment? Go around the group and give an example of when you have received a compliment and what this was like. Then give an example of when you have given a compliment and what this was like. What's the difference?

Is it easy or difficult to give or receive compliments? How often do you notice something about someone else? How do you think this would make them feel? How did we respond? For example, dismiss – "Oh no it's just an old jumper", accept – "Oh thanks" or ignore.

- Have the young people write a compliment for the person on their left and right. Go around the group, each reading out their compliments and giving them to them. They should then stick these on their paper bodies.

Equipment

- Worksheet
- Post-it notes
- Pens etc.
- Body outlines
- Present/star outlines/post-its to write/draw compliments.

Relaxation

What does your body feel/look like when it is relaxing? Progressive muscle relaxation

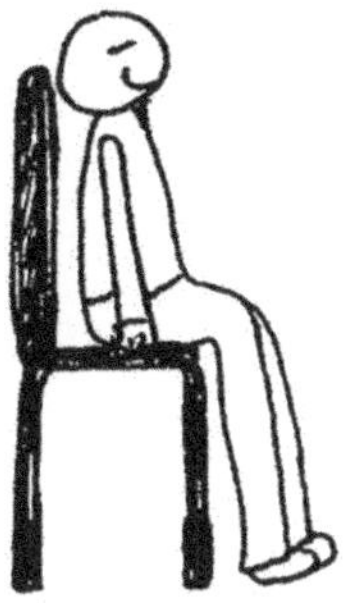

Aim

- To experience and practise relaxation activities to promote calmness and reduced tension.

Instructions

- **The scripts**: Use the script that matches the needs of your group. Try to use a relaxing voice, speaking slowly and using gentle rising and falling intonation. Leave short gaps in between sections; do not rush. Adjust your speed depending on how the group is reacting, e.g. if they need a more active approach leave less time or none in between sections to maintain their attention. These scripts are simply a guide, therefore adapt as appropriate to match the setting, young people and group. Hold tension for a few seconds and then release. Do not say the words in brackets – they are instructions for the facilitator.

  Feel free to use these scripts in different weeks so that the young people get used to doing progressive muscle relaxation. Remember, relaxation is a skill that is learned and needs to be practised.

- **Siting position**: If sitting, make sure their back and head are supported against the chair, or move chairs so that everyone has their head resting against the wall. Make sure everyone can have their feet flat on the floor. This will mean everyone's whole body will be well supported, comfortable and therefore more able to fully relax.

- **Environment**: Sometimes changing the environment, e.g. going into a more comfy room, a sensory room or a room with armchair-style chairs can shift the atmosphere to a more relaxing one. You could put on some quiet relaxing music or sounds, e.g. nature sounds, if that would be useful. You could close the curtains to cut out some light. You could consider using smell.

- **Before you start**: You could go through the movements before the session so they all know what to expect. Tell them about the script, including any details you think would be helpful for them to know before starting. Make sure they feel safe and that there will not be any interruptions and try to find a quiet environment. If there is noise, this is a good opportunity to block those sounds out and focus on the relaxation, as they may not always be able to find a quiet space in their own time. It's important to be able to relax in different environments. Make sure you tell the young people if they are finding it difficult or uncomfortable etc. that they can stop at any time, only doing what they feel comfortable with.

Note: Remember to seek medical advice before using progressive muscle relaxation (tensing and releasing/relaxing) with anyone who has heart problems.

If a young person is showing any signs of distress or any negative reaction, one staff member can offer to leave the room with them to help them while the rest of the group carry on.

If your students are deaf, then this relaxation can be done in the same way but with eyes open while copying the actions. Then closing eyes at the end while there is nothing to follow for a few moments.

Then invite them to close their eyes and enjoy the relaxation (if appropriate).

- **Introductory**: Ask them to sit comfortably on floor or chair.

Introductory Script, which may last just 1 minute or less at first:

1 Lie or sit comfortably. We are going to tense and relax different parts of the body. Squeeze muscles tight, hold, then release.

2 Lift your feet off the floor, bend your knees and tense the muscles in your legs. Hold this [for a few seconds]. Now release. Do this again. Lift your legs off the floor, hold [few seconds] now release.

3 Pull your tummy in and hold. Release. Do this again. Pull your tummy in, hold and release.

4 Make a fist and bend your arms, touching your hands on your shoulders. Tense the muscles in your hands and arms. Hold this. Now release back down. Do this again, make a fist and bend your arms, touching your hands on your shoulders. Now release your hands back to your sides or on your lap.

5 Shrug your shoulders up to your ears. Hold this. And let them fall down. For a second time shrug your shoulders up to your ears, hold. Then let them fall down.

6 Try to notice and remember how this feels to be relaxed. [Be silent for a few seconds if possible.]

7 Now gradually start to wiggle your fingers and toes. Wriggle on the chair. Start to notice the room and others around you and slowly, in your own time, open your eyes.

- **Developing**: Use yoga mats or the sensory room. Try various positions, e.g. sit upright with back supported or lie down on beanbag/mat.

Developing Script: 2–3 minutes:

1 Make yourself comfortable on the floor or chair/beanbag. We are going to tense and release different parts of the body to help us feel more relaxed.

2 When you release the tensed muscles, focus on the feeling of the muscles becoming relaxed and the tension drifting away.

3 Take a long slow breath in and out. Take another deep breath in, hold. Breathe out.

4 Now let's focus on our feet and legs. Curl your toes and bend your knees a little, tensing the muscles in your feet, lower legs and thighs. Hold this tension. Now release. Curl your toes and bend your knees a little, tensing the muscles in your feet and legs. Now release and let your legs go floppy and fall into a relaxed position.

5 Suck your tummy in, holding it tight with your belly button towards your spine. Then relax. Another time pull your tummy in hold and release. Feel the warm relaxation in your legs and tummy.

6 Take a deep slow breath in and hold this for a short time. Now release, let the breath flow out. Take a deep breath in, feel your muscles in your ribs tighten, then release.

7 Now make your hands into fists and move your hands to your shoulders, bending your elbows, tightening muscles in your arms and hands, hold, now release. Again tense your hands into fists, and tense your arms moving your hands to meet touch your shoulders. Hold this, and relax your hands onto your lap or the floor. Let them become floppy and relaxed. Feel the relaxation flowing down your arms.

8 Shrug your shoulders up to your ears, tensing the muscles in your back and shoulders. Hold here, keeping the tension. And let them fall down. For a second time shrug your shoulders up to your ears, hold. Then let them fall down releasing the tension in your shoulders.

9 Screw up your face tight. Hold this and relax. Once more, screw up your face and release.

10 Notice how your muscles and body feels now. Maybe warm, relaxed, floppy. Notice again where your body rests on the mat or chair. Feel yourself getting heavier with a sinking feeling gently in the floor or chair. Now I will be quiet. Enjoy the feeling of relaxation for a few moments.

11 [Be silent for a short time and allow the group to be relaxed for as much as the young people can tolerate; when they start moving or opening their eyes, move on.]

12 Now gradually start to wiggle your fingers and toes. Wriggle on the chair. Start to notice the room and others around you and slowly in your own time open your eyes.

- **Experienced** – Ask the group members to find their most comfortable and relaxing sitting position. This can be extended to lying down/standing up. Link this to breathing exercises.

Ask them to tense individual arts of their body, and then relax them. Afterwards ask them how this felt, what they noticed, e.g. warm, relaxed, soft etc. Was this a nice feeling? They can do this in bed at night to help them fall asleep if they find that difficult.

Experienced Script: 4–6 minutes:

1 We are going to tense and release different parts of the body to help us feel more relaxed and release any tension in our muscles. When you release the tensed muscles, focus on the feeling of the muscles becoming relaxed and the tension drifting away.

2 Make yourself comfortable on the floor or chair/beanbag with your back and head supported. Notice where your body rests on the mat or chair. [Leave a few seconds for this.]

3 Take a long slow breath in and out. Do this a few more times at your own pace. [Leave some time to do this when the young people have taken two or three breaths.]

4 Now focus on your feet. Curl your toes and tense the muscles in your feet. Hold these tight for a few moments. Now release. Again curl your toes and tense your feet, hold [wait] and release.

5 Tense the muscles in your lower legs, pushing them into the chair or floor. Hold this. Then release. Do this again, tense your lower legs and push them into the floor or chair, hold and release.

6 Tense the muscles in your thighs and legs, pushing your legs down into the chair/mat. Hold this. Then release. Another time, let's tense the muscles in your thighs and legs, pushing your legs into the chair/mat. Hold this. Then release. Feel the relaxation in your legs. [Wait.]

7 Move your focus to your tummy. Suck your tummy in, holding it tight. Then relax. Again, pull your tummy in with your belly button towards your spine, hold and release. Feel the warm relaxation in your legs and tummy.

8 Take a deep slow breath in and hold this for a short time. Now release, let the breath flow out. Take a deep breath in, feel your muscles in your ribs tighten, then release.

9 Now make your hands into fists, clench them tight, then release. Again tense your hands into fists, hold this, and relax your hands.

10 Move your hands to your shoulders, bending your elbows and tighten the muscles in your arms. Hold this. Then release your hands down. Again tighten the muscles in your arms moving your hands to your shoulders. Hold. And release down, resting your hands on your lap or the floor. Feel the relaxation flowing down your arms.

11 Shrug your shoulders up to your ears, tensing the muscles in your back and shoulders. Hold here keeping the tension. And let them fall down. Do this again, shrug your shoulders up to your ears, hold. Then let them fall down, releasing the tension in your shoulders.

12 Screw up your face tight. Hold this and relax. Once more, screw up your face and release.

13 Notice how your muscles and body feel now. Maybe warm, relaxed, floppy or heavy. Notice again where your body rests on the mat or chair. Feel yourself getting heavier with a sinking feeling gently in the floor or chair. Now I will be quiet. Enjoy the feeling of relaxation for a few moments.

14 [Be silent for a few moments and allow the group to be relaxed.]

15 Now gradually start to wiggle your fingers and toes. Wriggle on the chair. Start to notice the room and others around you and slowly in your own time open your eyes.

Equipment

- Chairs or mats to lie on
- Sensory room if big enough
- Relaxation activities sheet/bodies for each young person to add activities they like/how their body feels

Talking Points related to this session

- Different people have different needs.
- We aren't all good at everything.
- Everyone is different and that's ok – learn to love yourself.

Session 3 Colour

Mindfulness

Colouring a shape

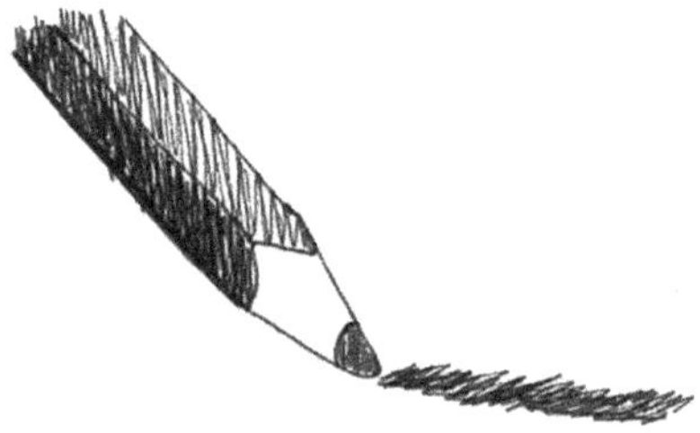

Aims

- To experience and practise being in the moment, focusing on the here and now.

Instructions

- Choose a colour, type of tool (chalk, oil pastel, felt tip pen, pencil etc.) and colour a shape in – concentrate on how the pencil feels in your hand, how the pencil feels on the paper, the colouring going bigger/smaller, where is it on the page. Focus on the repetitive action of colouring, the feeling of the tool in your hand and on the paper etc.
- **Introductory**: Ask them to choose a favourite colour, colour in the shape.
- **Developing**: Ask them to colour a simple picture.
- **Experienced**: Ask them to choose a colour which represents their mood at the moment.
- In a discussion after this activity, ask them: How did this feel in your hand? What happened to your mind? Why did you choose the colour or the shape?

Equipment

- Paper
- Blank outlines of shapes
- Colouring pencils/crayons/paint

Identity

What do different colours mean to me?

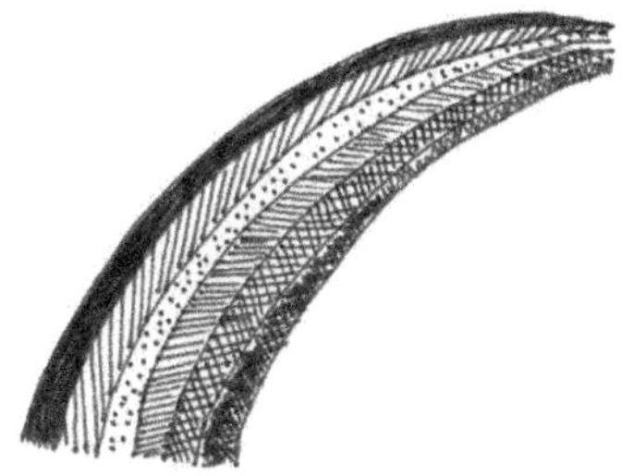

Aim

- To think what colours mean to you and other people. To link emotions/things with colours.

Instructions

- **Introductory**: Which colours represent things in my life? For example, colour of school, colour of hair, colour of football team, colour of clothes today. Draw these and put them on the paper bodies. They can be different outfits for different roles around the body rather than on it.
- **Developing**: Which colours represent me? For example, colours representing a range of everyday concrete things (as for Introductory activity above) and abstract things (feelings, moods, facial expression pictures).
- **Experienced**: Which colours are important to me? Why? Which colours describe me? Which colours represent personalities, emotions?

Equipment

- Pictures/pencils of different colours

Self-esteem

What is my favourite colour and why?

Aim

- To feel a sense of achievement.

Instructions

- **Introductory**: Go around and say your favourite colour. Have different coloured pens/crayons/felt tips and colouring activity available, name positive behaviours, e.g. good colouring/focus/praise for others, encourage naming of positive behaviours in others.
- **Developing**: Go around and say your favourite colour. Staff members model choosing and discussing their favourite colours and take the lead with colour chart available for reference. Link the colour to positive memories of items in your favourite colour. You could plot a bar chart with favourite colours on the white board.
- **Experienced**: Go around and say your favourite colour and why. Have a discussion about which colours are linked to a range of memories and feelings of success. Discuss how wearing certain colours can alter or add to your self-esteem.
- Create a short poem, drawing or paragraph of your favourite colour and why it is so important to you.

Equipment

- Colour chart, e.g. paint colours
- Colouring activity – pencils/pens, paper

Relaxation

Visualising colours

Aims

- To experience and practise relaxation activities to promote calmness and reduced tension.
- To visualise a colour in their mind. They could choose something of that colour from pictures or objects.
- Visualise breathing in blue (or a calming colour) and breathing out red.

Instructions

- **Introductory**: Use a parachute type activity; sit under the parachute and pick out a colour to look at as it drifts over you. Feel the wind on your skin. You could use breathing in as the parachute rises and out as it falls. Or visualise breathing in and out different colours as the parachute goes up and down.
- **Developing**: Use the shape that was coloured in from the start of the session and picture that in your mind.
- **Experienced**: Visualisation, no props. Think of a bubble of the chosen colour. Link this to your breathing and it circulating around your body. Keep going until you feel bathed in your chosen colour.

Equipment

- Parachute

Talking Points related to this session

- Different people have different needs.
- We aren't all good at everything.
- Everyone is different and that's ok – learn to love yourself.

Activity sheets for session 3 – Colours and Emotions

Colour	Emotion
Blue	
Green	
Red	
Orange	
Yellow	
Purple	

Colour	Role
	School
	Sports team
	Youth group
	Religious place

Colour	Emotion
	Happy
	Sad
	Angry
	Worried
	Frustrated

T-shirt outlines

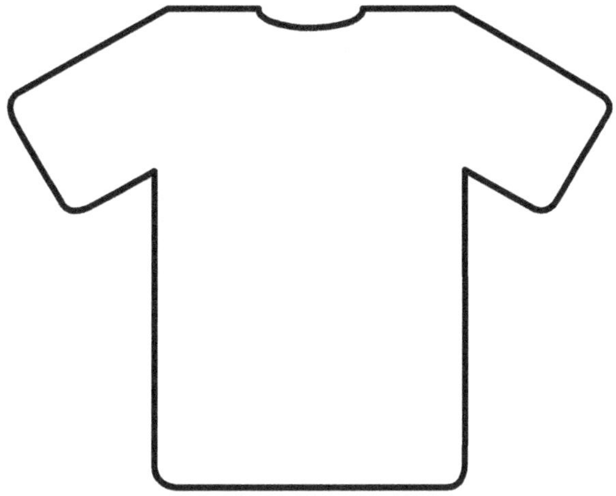

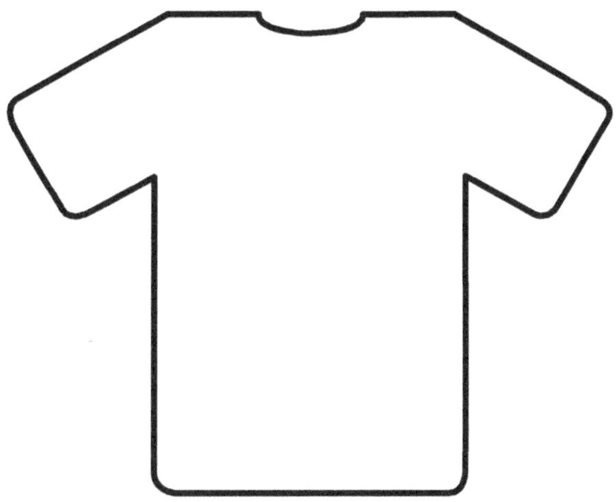

School name –

Age –

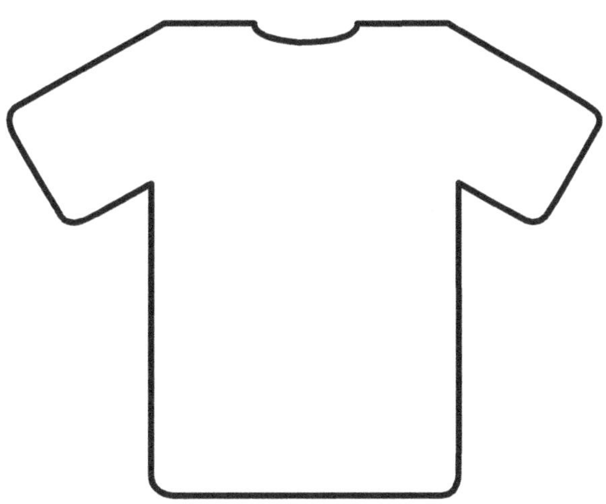

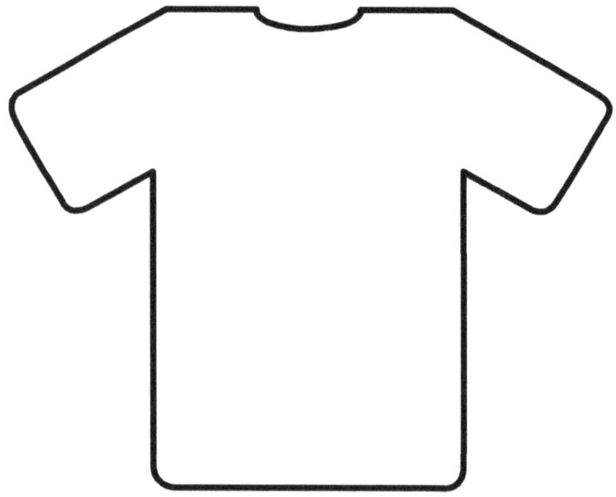

School name –

Age –

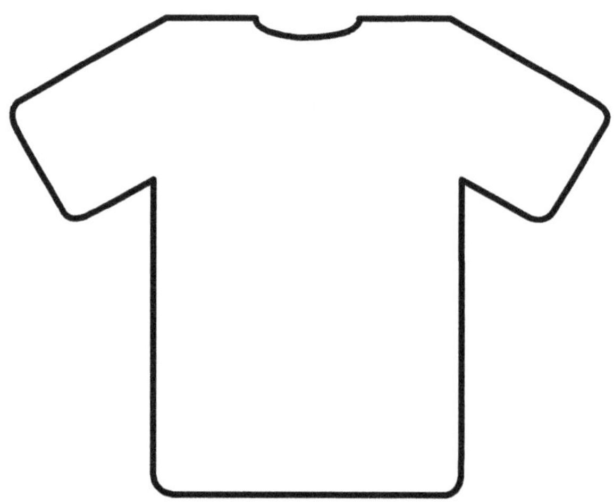

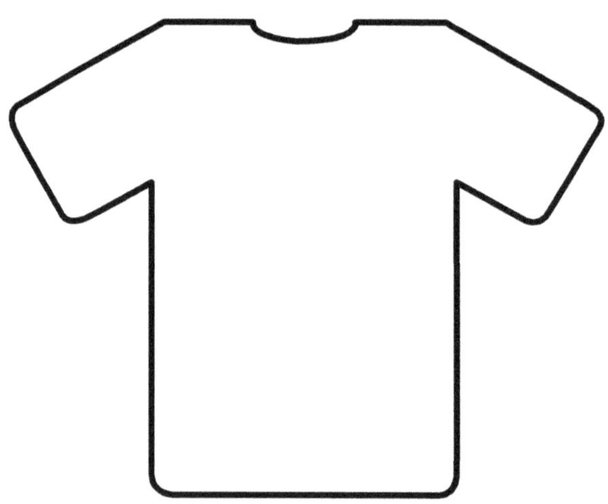

School name –

Age –

Session 4 Senses: sound, vibration and smell

Mindfulness

Use a sensory object to feel mindfully

Do finger painting mindfully

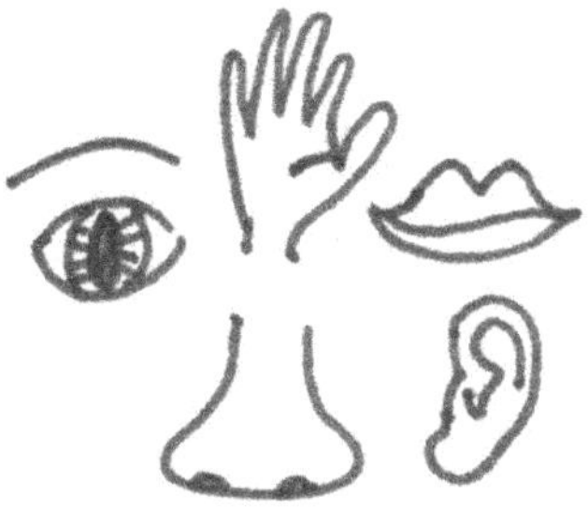

Aim

- To experience and practise being in the moment, focusing on the here and now.

Instructions

- Choose a sensory object (spike ball, light ball, different type of textured fabric, vibrating cushion, smell [oil] etc.) and focus on using your senses.

OR

- Choose a colour paint to do some finger painting or painting with your hands. Encourage young people to focus on how the paint feels and the experience of doing this. You could use scented paints to enhance the experience and add another sense in.
- Focus on the object or finger painting for the amount of time decided.
- Discuss your experience as you feel comfortable.
- Focus again.
- **Introductory**: Liked or didn't like it. They could then choose some of these sensory experiences and write or draw them. Stick them to the paper bodies near the sense organs they relate to.
- **Developing**: Liked it/didn't like it because. . . . Draw what the objects and textures feel like. Describe the feeling, supporting each other to use and understand new words or signs, e.g. comfortable, uncomfortable, relaxing, irritating, tense, soothing, calming etc.
- **Experienced**: Discuss experience of object and being mindful. Were you able to focus for the whole time? How did you feel?

Equipment

- Different textured fabric or balls
- Different sound makers
- Different smells of oils
- Vibrating cushion

Identity

Things I love and hate and the bits in between. My preferences.

Stages of don't like, like and love

Aims

- Encourage an awareness of stages between love and hate, preferences and how good you are at a variety of different things.
- Call out various objects, foods, activities etc. and ask them to rate how much they love or hate these by standing somewhere on the line/continuum around the room. Try to make some of these related to the senses. Some examples:
    - Bathing to relax
    - Hand writing
    - Watching or playing football or other sports or games
    - Going to school

Instructions

Continuums

- Like/don't like
- Preferences
- Love (1) to hate (10)

There are lists of ideas for these and posters in the activity sheets at the end of this session.

Encourage consideration of grades between extremes, therefore encouraging flexible thinking and discouraging black-and-white thinking. There will be a variety of abilities in this depending on the level of the young people. Consider how this might change in different situations. For example, you might hate spiders, but if they're eating mosquitos so they're not biting you, you might like/appreciate them then, but not when they are crawling on you.

If possible, add in trying different things, smells or tastes, and making a decision whether they like them or not, e.g. different essential oils, things from the kitchen, shower gel etc. Young people could be asked to bring in something they like the smell of.

- **Introductory**: What things do they like? Stick up 'like' and 'don't like' posters on the walls on each side of the room. Call out things they may or may not like and have the young people go to the poster that reflects whether they like it or not. You may be able to bring 'it's ok' in the middle or degrees of how much they like this. Have a quick discussion about some of these. Then ask the young people to come up with their own ideas and call them out.

And/or try preferences. For example, have them go to one side of the room if they prefer a beach or the other side if they prefer a pool.

- **Developing**: Have two extremes on the floor – love and hate – and stick a line of masking tape to the floor in between linking them like a continuum with a mark in the middle. This could also be done by taping a ribbon or masking tape on a table if there is a lack of space. Explain that it is a continuum. Check whether young people know what this means. Ask what would be in the middle, i.e. like. Young people go to a place on the continuum representing how much they like something. They can be given the opportunity to call out their own ideas. Add in words for bits in between if they can. Briefly discuss these words in between.
- **Experienced**: Put numbers 1–10 around the room, on the floor or on the table in sequence. The young people go to the number that represents how they feel about the particular thing when they are called out. Have a brief discussion about why young people have chosen that place and any stories they want to share. Then invite young people to call out their own.

Self-esteem

What senses do

Using our senses to help us relax

Aims

- Record the preferences from the identity activity on the paper bodies.
- Explore the different senses of touch, sound and smell through objects.
- Young people can think about how they can their use their senses to feel more relaxed: 'Things that make me feel relaxed.'

Instructions

- **All**: From the identity activity, write or draw one or more of the things that make you feel good about yourself. Attach these to the paper bodies.

AND/OR

- Explore the different senses of touch, sound and smell through objects. Try different things and choose some you like and/or help you feel good or relaxed or comforted. Use different textures of fabric, different smells, e.g. oils, or different genres of music.
- These could be things bought from home, e.g. teddy, comfort blanket, photo, book etc.
- **Introductory**: Use two objects in each sense and pass these around the group. Ask them which they prefer. Choose their favourite of all the objects.
- **Developing**: Go around the group and encourage young people to explain a smell that they like. Note any similarities and differences promoting/modelling a non-judgemental, accepting and open manner.

- **Experienced**: Have a variety of objects representing each sense and have the young people explore them freely, one sense at a time. Choose the ones they like best in each sense and record these on the 'Be good to yourself' worksheet.

OR

What things help you feel relaxed in everyday life, either when you are stressed/tense or everyday things? Remember that being happy helps us feel less tense and reduces stress, so doing things that make us happy more often may help us feel more relaxed.

Questions to use in a discussion.

- What music do you like?
- What music do you find relaxing? What makes it relaxing? Play different music and ask the young person to rate how relaxed they felt.
- Is feeling the rhythm and beat of the music in the chair relaxing?
- Do the speed or type of music make a difference?
- What does relaxation feel like in your body (e.g. soft muscles, slower heart rate, warm, clear mind etc.)?
- Choose textures that are relaxing, e.g. fur etc., link to stroking an animal.
- Choose objects that are relaxing. Complete worksheet or write or draw their preferences.

Note: Young people could be invited prior to the group to bring things in that they find relaxing, e.g. a piece of music, something to feel and their favourite smell. Parents, carers and staff may be able to support young people in doing this.

Equipment

- Sensory room
- Scale of love to hate
- Different textures and sensory objects
- 'Be good to yourself' form OR
- Relaxing smells, textures and sounds worksheet
- What does relaxation feel like in my body information from Session 2

Relaxation

Use your senses to help you to relax

Music, sound and touch

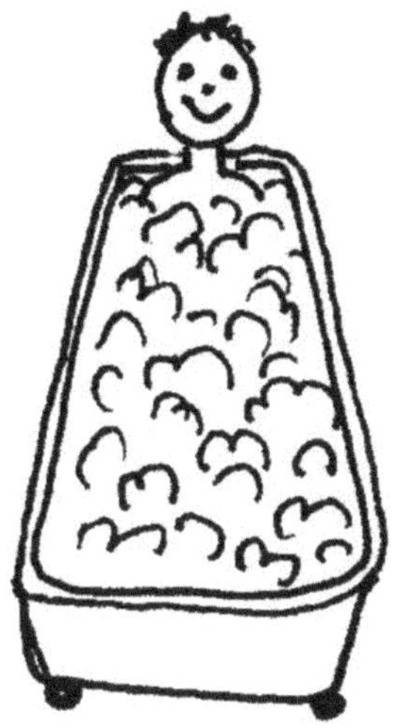

Aim

- To experience and practise relaxation activities to promote calmness and reduced tension.

Instructions

- If you have another room, set it up before the activity to make a quiet space. This could be with curtains or blinds down to darken the room. Have lamps for soft lighting, big cushions, yoga mats or comfy chairs to sit or lie on. Have some relaxation music ready.
- Ask the young people to get comfy and sit or lie somewhere. Let them know that you will be playing relaxation music. When the music finishes, the relaxation will finish. Then have a few minutes to discuss their experiences and reacclimatise.
- Vary the length of time or type of music, dependent on your group.
- If the young people are deaf, choose sensory objects to feel, see, smell and focus on.
- **Introductory**: Young people choose an object or sound from the previous mindfulness or self-esteem activity. They can use this to help them relax.
- **Developing**: As above, plus complete a 'Be good to yourself form'/list of liked activities for relaxation. They should think about what things they like doing and what things they are good at, linked with their senses.
- **Experienced**: Complete first two activities and recap key features of each person's relaxation; include relaxed muscles in the body and relaxed breathing.
- Choose a relaxing activity and plan a few times in the week when they will do this.

Talking Points related to this session

- Managing difficulties in life.
- Promote healthy lifestyles.
- Coping with difficulties.
- Managing feelings.
- Different people have different needs.
- We aren't all good at everything.
- Everyone is different and that's ok – learn to love yourself.

Activity sheets for session 4

Colour Resources

List of preferences

- Relaxing in a bath or shower
- Beach or swimming pool
- Going to the dentist or doctor
- Marmite or peanut butter on toast
- Holding a frog or snail
- Having a picnic or barbeque
- Snowball fight or water fight
- Blue or green/red or yellow/pink or blue etc.
- When upset, a hug or talking
- A variety of smells

List of things that you might be good at

- Handwriting
- Playing football or other sports
- Telling jokes
- Making people laugh
- Using a knife and fork
- Drawing
- Making things
- Fixing things
- Problem solving
- Maths
- Science

- A foreign language
- Being a good friend
- Being kind/helpful/thoughtful etc. (characteristics)

List of things to love, like, hate

- Marmite
- Spiders
- Dark
- Walking
- Running
- Sports (specify)
- Eating peas, carrots or oranges etc.
- Takeaway food
- Salad
- Going out
- Youth club
- Watching films/TV
- Cooking
- How much are you enjoying the mindfulness activities?
- A variety of smells, e.g. the smell of grass being cut, melting chocolate, rubbish etc.
- Variety of music genres: classical, rock, jazz, pop, RnB, hip hop etc.

Love	**Like**	**Hate**
1	1	1
2	2	2
3	3	3
4	4	4
5	5	5

Things that help me feel less tense

When can I use these? Draw lines to link the strategies to situations

Fun things that help me feel relaxed	When do I do these?

Be good to yourself

My relaxing smells, textures and sounds: Developing worksheet

Sense	**What I like/What is relaxing**
Sound	
Smell	
Movement	
Touch	
Taste	
See	

Be good to yourself

My relaxing smells, textures and sounds: Experienced worksheet

Sense	What I like/What is relaxing	How does it makes me feel? When can I use this to help me relax?
Sound		
Smell		
Movement		
Touch		
Taste		
See		

Self-soothing – things that make me feel good

Vision	Sound	Taste	Movement	Smell	Touch

Session 5 Food – what do I like?

Mindfulness

Eating a Malteser or raisin mindfully

Aim

- To experience and practise being in the moment, focusing on the here and now.

Instructions

- Explain the whole mindfulness exercise first. Eat a raisin or Malteser mindfully. Then while doing the exercise, explain the stages.
- Here are some helpful questions to ask:

1 Look at the Malteser – what does it look like? What does it smell like? What does it feel like?

2 Put it in your mouth, but don't chew on it – just let it melt. Notice the feelings of it on the tongue, in the mouth. Where is it? What does it feel like?

3 Notice where the Malteser is in the body, in the mouth, in the throat going down to the stomach. . .

Change the language and detail according to the level.

- **Introductory**: Using the pictures for each stage of the process (as above): (1) look, (2) hold in mouth, (3) swallow (discuss where it goes if needed). Get one piece of feedback from each group member describing their experience or something they noticed.
- **Developing**: Describe and complete the process. Get feedback from each person to add to the board.
- **Experienced**: Try different foods, e.g. a raisin and then a Malteser and compare them. Describe similarities and differences when sharing at the end.

Equipment

- Choice of food: Malteser, raisin, After Eight, chocolate orange segment, Polo

Identity

What foods do I like?

Aims

- To name foods I like.
- To think about how others may like different foods.

Instructions

- **Introductory**: Show pictures of basic foods (milk, toast, cereal, squash) for the young people to pick out their favourites and stick on their paper bodies. They could draw the foods they like on the plate outline worksheet, cut them out and stick them to their paper bodies.
- **Developing**: Show pictures of a variety of foods. Describe their favourite food and a time that they have eaten it, e.g. on holiday, in a restaurant, Sunday lunch at home etc. Decide if food is made or grown or has ingredients in it that are grown. And if it is grown, how? For example, is it grown underground (potato), on the ground (pumpkin) or in a tree (apple)? You could have different pictures illustrating this, e.g. a simple picture of a bush, tree and roots could be drawn.
- **Experienced**: Describe their favourite food and a time that they have eaten it, e.g. on holiday, in a restaurant, Sunday lunch at home etc. What happened? Who was there?

Equipment

- Pictures of different foods
- Picture of food grown on, under or above ground
- Map of the world for reference

Self-esteem

What can I cook?

Aims

- Think of things that I can cook.
- To feel a sense of achievement that they can cook something, however simple.

Instructions

- **Introductory**: Draw a picture of something that they can help make (toast, a drink, boiled egg, cakes).
- **Developing**: Draw or discuss what they have made in the past or what they would like to make. Discuss steps to take to achieve that. Write this on a sequence board: 'I can cook. . . '.
- **Experienced**: Discussion: What is their speciality? Who have they cooked for before? What ingredients do they need? Describe a time when you have made something and how it went. Have you made this for others? Describe this. Write out how to make it or draw a picture of it to put on the paper bodies.

Equipment

- Paper, pencils/pens

Relaxation

Spaghetti – cooked and raw illustrating tension and relaxation in the body

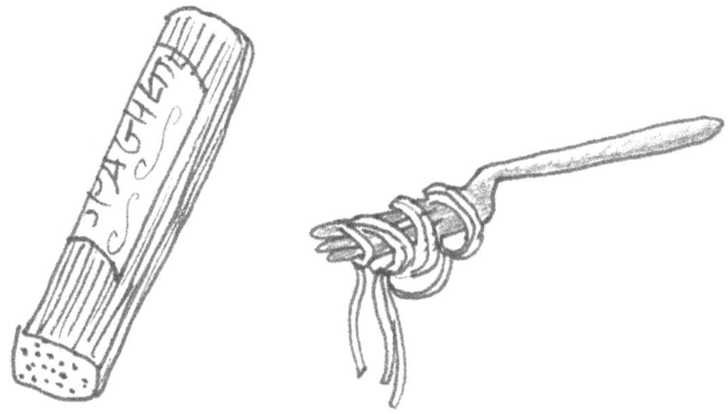

Aims

- To experience and practise relaxation activities to promote calmness and reduced tension.
- To learn about the different between tension and relaxation in muscles.

Instructions

- This relaxation is more psycho-educational, i.e. exploring the difference between tension and relaxation rather than practising a relaxation activity in itself.
- Have the young people look at the difference between the cooked and raw spaghetti and describe the difference between the two. Guide a discussion linking these to the state of our bodies when they feel tense and relaxed. How can we help our bodies feel more like cooked spaghetti?
- You might want to go to a kitchen and cook some spaghetti in the group. A tip is to have someone make sure the water is boiling before and everything is set up to save time. Otherwise, cook the spaghetti before and bring it in so the group can see and feel it.
- **Introductory**: Ask the young people to feel the cooked and dry spaghetti and describe what they feel like. Ask them to stand upright like a cooked or raw spaghetti and then floppy like a piece of cooked spaghetti. They may want to demonstrate being floppy by lying on the floor on mats. Pick up the arm of each young person lying on the floor. If they are relaxed, their arms should flop back down to the floor. Explain that you are going to do this and encourage them to make themselves floppy and relaxed like the cooked spaghetti.
- **Developing**: Do the above. Describe the difference and relate this to tension and relaxation in the body/muscles. You could introduce more foods. Ask the young people to introduce their own ideas of opposites that are soft and tough/hard.

- **Experienced**: Ask the young people to imagine their muscles/body like a piece of raw spaghetti. Whilst seated or lying on the floor, have them tense their body like a piece of solid spaghetti. Then ask them to imagine a piece of cooked floppy spaghetti and let their muscles go to become like floppy spaghetti. Do the above and ask the young people to introduce their own ideas and lead the group in a short relaxation exercise. Have them notice the difference in body movements and how this can help to relax. They could use different parts of the body for different foods.

Equipment

- Cooked spaghetti
- Raw spaghetti
- Floor mats

Talking Points related to this session

- Different people have different needs.
- We aren't all good at everything.
- Everyone is different and that's ok – learn to love yourself.
- Working towards your own life goals.

Activity sheets for session 5

Food I like plates

I can cook resource

Step 1	Step 2	Step 3
Step 4	Step 5	Step 6

Words to describe tension and relaxation

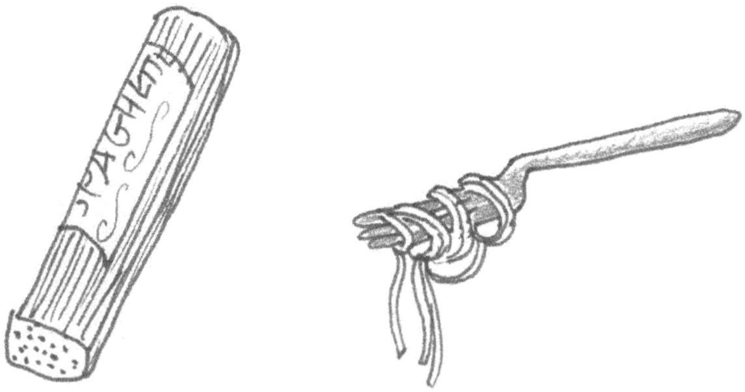

Stiff Firm Solid Flexible Supple

Hard Rigid Tough Elastic Stretchy

Snaps easily Brittle Soft Bendy Squishy Spongy Pliable

Think of words and signs to describe relaxation and tension. Practise these with your body.

Session 6 Food from around the world

Mindfulness

World fruit – Eating fruit mindfully

Aim

- To experience and practise being in the moment, focusing on the here and now.

Instructions

- Explain the whole mindfulness exercise and stages first. Eat the fruit mindfully. Then while doing the exercise, explain the stages as instructions.
- **All**: Stages/instructions:
    1. Look and feel the whole fruit/piece of fruit. What does it look like? What does it smell like? What does it feel like?
    2. Put it in your mouth but don't chew it – just let it melt. What does it feel like in your mouth? Notice the feelings of it on the tongue, in the mouth. Where is it? What does it feel like? What does it taste like? Does this change?
    3. Notice where the fruit is in the body, in the mouth, and as you swallow and how it feels in the throat and going down to the stomach.
- Change the language and detail according to the ability.
- Discuss this in the group. Go round and ask each what their experience was.

Equipment

- Fruit: mango, melon (different types), banana, orange, apple, pear, papaya etc. (if not in season, these could be tinned fruit in juice not syrup, as that is extra sugar).
- Different fruits cut up into mouth-size pieces.
- Cup/plate/bowl to put the fruit on.

Identity

What foods do I like from different countries?

Aims

- Consider what foods you like from around the world/different countries.
- Match foods to the countries/climates they are grown in.
- Think about how others may like different foods.
- Learn about and share the different types of foods from different cultures and religions around the world, considering the similarities and differences to your own.

Instructions

- As always, pick the activities that suit your group and use as many or few as you need, as there are a few options within this element.
- **Introductory**:
  - Show pictures of basic foods from other countries for them to pick out.
  - Play a game; call out categories and the young people point at the food in that category; countries or types of foods, favourite foods, foods they hate, food grown underground etc. Pictures of different foods could be stuck around the room and they move to these when categories are called out.
  - Pictures of foods could be sorted into different categories.
  - Favourite world foods could then be drawn or stuck on paper bodies as time allows.
- **Developing**: Show pictures of a variety of foods (or have some different foods): fruits and vegetables and whole dishes/meals. These could be brought in from home.
  - Match the food to the country of origin. You could check on the label where it is grown/made. The same food may grow in different countries, therefore think about the climates that certain foods need to grow, e.g. bananas won't grow in the UK. On a world map, cut out and stick where the different foods are grown.

- Cut out/draw/write your favourite foods and stick them to your paper bodies or the country of origin. If the map is small, stick the food around the edge and draw lines, use thin ribbon to link the food with the place.

- **Experienced**: A discussion can be held around different foods they eat from different countries. Link foods to different cultures and practices. Young people could bring in food from their own culture or pictures of dishes and describe how it is made and when it is eaten, e.g. at a special event. If food is brought in, it could be shared with the group as appropriate. Examples of different food practices in different cultures (research more as required):
    - Some countries people eat with their hands or chopsticks, some people sit on the floor, some use leaves as plates, some people are vegetarian or vegan.
    - The same foods can be grown in different places.
    - Religion and food: food used in temples left for gods, church for communion, offerings to gods in temples etc.
    - Match food to the countries on a world map. This could also be linked with religion.
    - Are there foods from your or your parent's/grandparent's country of origin that you like/don't like?
    - Invite young people to share stories about food from different countries. This may need to be prompted with examples.

Equipment

- Pictures of different foods (meals/dishes and whole foods, e.g. fruit and veg), food labels, words/flags of different countries
- Map of the world for reference
- String/ribbon to match food to countries
- Young people could be invited the previous week to bring food from their culture/religion if appropriate.

Self-esteem

Making smoothies

Aims

- To feel a sense of achievement that they can make something, however simple.
- To try something new.

Instructions

- **Introductory**: Taste smoothies prepared by others, or put prepared fruit into a blender to design your own smoothie.
- **Developing**: Make a smoothie with staff support to wash, peel and cut the fruit as appropriate, therefore completing more of the process from the introductory level.
- **Experienced**: Invent, write recipe and make your own smoothie.
- **All**: Draw/write the smoothie that you like in the glass and stick this on your body outline.

Equipment

- Fruits from around the world
- Milk/yoghurt

- Fruit juice
- Blender
- Glasses, two or three each to try different smoothies
- Worksheet – outline of smoothie glass
- Pens and colouring pens/pencils etc.
- Glue
- Glass outline worksheet
- Body outlines

Relaxation

Relaxation: Be a celery, be a lettuce

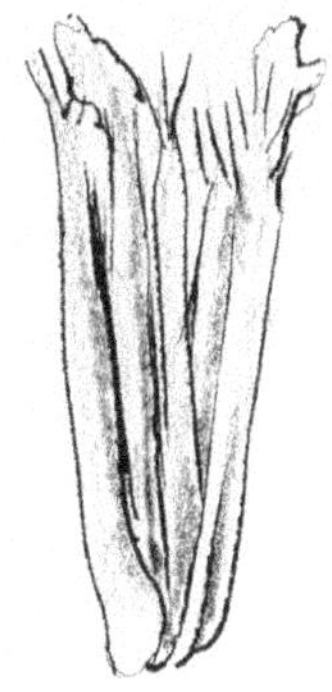

Aim

- To experience and practise relaxation activities to promote calmness and reduced tension.

Instructions

- Use the progressive muscle relaxation scripts from Session 2 relaxation if you feel this would be helpful.
- **Introductory**: Ask the young people to feel the lettuce and celery and describe what they feel like. Ask them to stand upright like a celery stick and go floppy like a lettuce leaf. They may want to demonstrate being floppy by lying on the floor on mats. Pick up the arm of each young person one by one lying on the floor. If they are relaxed, their arms should flop back down to the floor. Be careful to do this on a soft mat so they don't bump their arm on the floor. Explain that you are going to do this and check that it's ok first. Encourage them to make themselves floppy and relaxed like the lettuce.
- **Developing**: Do the above. Describe the difference and relate this to tension and relaxation in the body/muscles. You could introduce more foods. Ask the young people to introduce their own ideas of opposites that are soft and tough/hard.
- **Experienced**: Ask the young people to imagine their muscles/body like a piece of celery or raw spaghetti. Whilst seated or lying on the floor, have them tense their body like a piece of solid celery or spaghetti. Then ask them to imagine a piece of cooked lettuce or floppy spaghetti and let their muscles go to become like lettuce or floppy spaghetti. Do the above and ask the young people to introduce their own ideas and lead the group in a short relaxation exercise. Have them notice the difference in body movements and how this can help to relax. They could use different parts of the body for different foods. Encourage them to think about what their body feels like when it is relaxed and when it is tense. By noticing the difference, in everyday life they can identify when they are feeling tense, which will help them relax more.

Note: This activity is similar to the one in the 'foods I like' topic with the cooked and uncooked spaghetti. This is a good follow on as the previous week was more psycho-educational and this week is more practical. Refer back to the spaghetti analogy to help with their learning.

Equipment

- A lettuce and sticks of celery are best, but a picture will do
- Pictures of different soft/floppy and hard crunchy foods they can use for inspiration

Talking Points related to this session

- Everyone is different and that's ok – learn to love yourself.
- Promote healthy lifestyles.
- Different people have different needs.
- Persevering.

Activity sheets for session 6

Under/on and above ground

Above ground

On ground

Under ground

Self-esteem

What can I make?

Smoothie

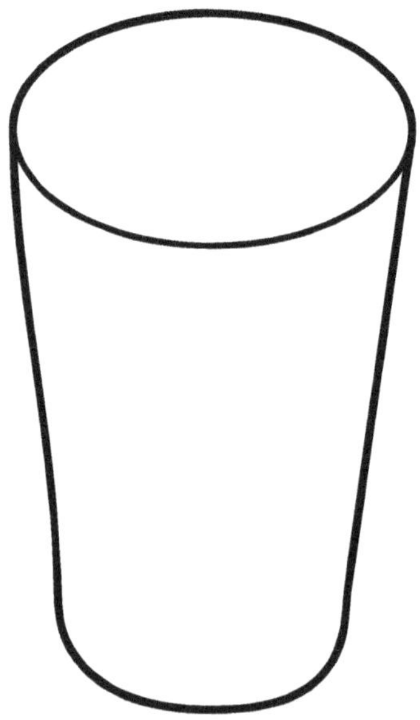

- What goes in the smoothie?
- Where does it grow? How does it grow? (bush, tree, in the ground etc.)
- What does it taste like?
- Do you like it?

Session 7 Clothes – what do I like?

Mindfulness

Feel different textures of fabric mindfully

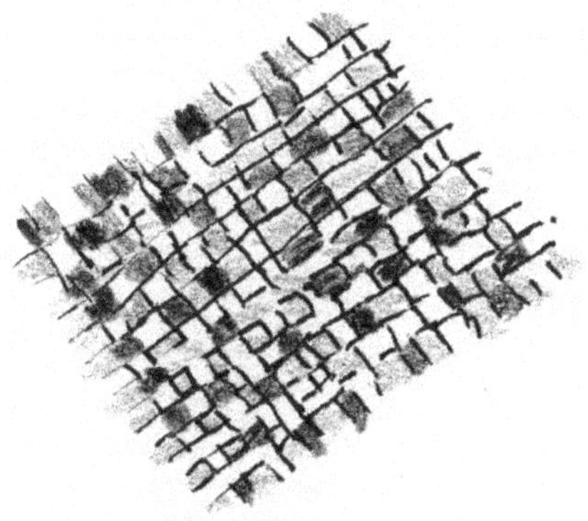

Aim

- To experience and practise being in the moment, focusing on the here and now.

Instructions

- Have a collection of different textures and colours of fabric. Often people have fabric at home they could give to the group or sewing shops may have off cuts, so ask around.
- Encourage the young people to choose a piece of fabric that they like the feel of by trying out the different ones. It may therefore be worth having a few cuts of each fabric.

1 Feel the fabric on your hands, on your face or arm and look at it for the time given.

2 Go around in the group and discuss your experience and how you found it etc.

3 Feel the fabric again. You can choose a different fabric if they wish.

4 Go around in the group and discuss your experience and how you found it etc. Was it different the second time around?

OR

- Mindfulness game: Make a vocabulary word list from the colours, textures, and any associations that the different fabrics bring. Everyone is thinking about the fabric and the words will come up from this. Go around the room and complete words beginning with each letter of the alphabet, e.g. A = apricot coloured, B = bristly, C = cuddly/reminds me of a cat etc.

Equipment

- Different fabrics

Identity

What do your clothes say about you?

Aim

- To think about what our clothes say about us as a person.

Instructions

- **Introductory**:
    - Ask the young people to look at the clothes they have on and say which item is their favourite. Or ask them to describe their favourite clothes and when they would wear these.
    - Have pictures of different types of clothes. Match clothes to activities, e.g. sports clothes to a sport, a suit to work etc. as a group on the worksheet, which could be printed A4 or A3 size.
- **Developing**:
    - Explain the choice of clothes they have on and how it reflects on them as a person, e.g. laid back, practical, clever, sporty etc.
    - If this is too personal or school uniforms are worn, the young people could look through magazines or newspapers and cut out pictures of people in different types of clothes. Go around and say what that says about the person wearing them, what they do (in a football kit = likes football, but do they like watching or playing or both? We don't know.), where they live. Be careful to challenge stereotypes thoughtfully here and reinforce that you cannot tell what someone's personality is from their appearance. The worksheet can be used if this is helpful to give structure.
- **Experienced:**
    - What do clothes in general say about people (e.g. business suits, uniforms, casual, smart, bright, dark, baggy, tight etc.)? Look at different pictures of people wearing different clothes. What do you think of when you see these pictures? Challenge stereotypes that everyone makes about someone else's appearance.

- What do your clothes say about you? Yes, we shouldn't make stereotypes about people, but it does happen. Does this match your character? Does this match how you want to come across to others?

Equipment

- Pictures of different clothes items

Self-esteem

Make a hat and add some qualities you have and some you want

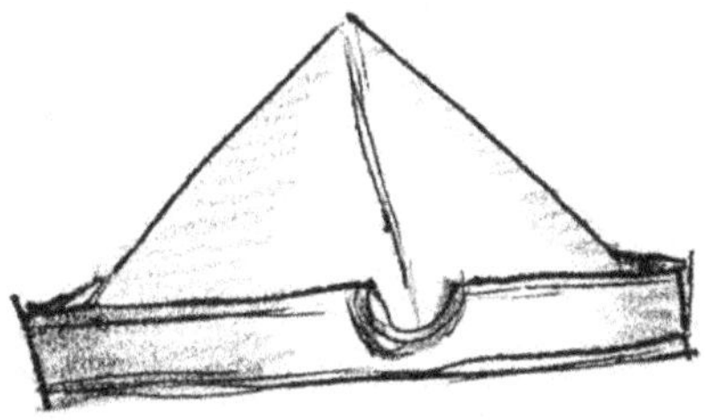

Aim

- To start a project and finish it the best they can with a sense of achievement that can be extended to other projects.

Instructions

- **Introductory**: Give the young people a cut out template to make a hat. Ask them to decorate; colour and stick things on (depending on the resources you have) the hat and then put it together.
- **Developing**: Have them draw a hat on their paper bodies. Write words on it that describe them. Use the discussions in the previous activity to help young people think about their characteristics, but more about personality will be added, as you can't tell someone's personality from what they look like.
- **Experienced**: Complete the worksheets individually. Staff to go around and help young people as necessary. Share with the group after.

Characteristics I have now	Characteristics I want/ What do I want to be like?	What do I want to do in the future? What characteristics do I need to be able to reach my goal, e.g. work/college?

Equipment

- Fabric
- Paper
- Cardboard
- Stapler (with care)
- Scissors (with care)
- Pencils/pens
- Needle and thread (with care)

Relaxation

How do your clothes feel on your body?

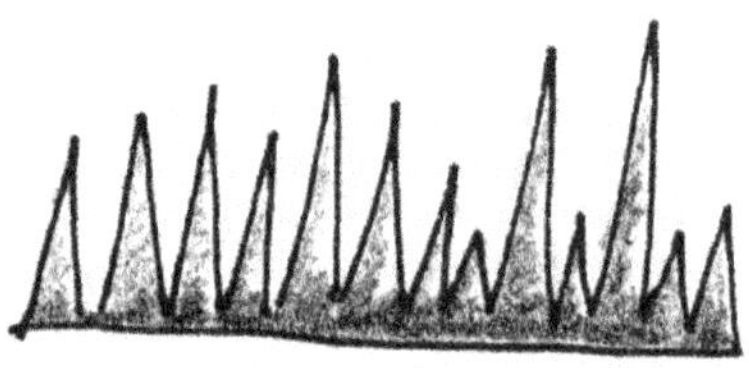

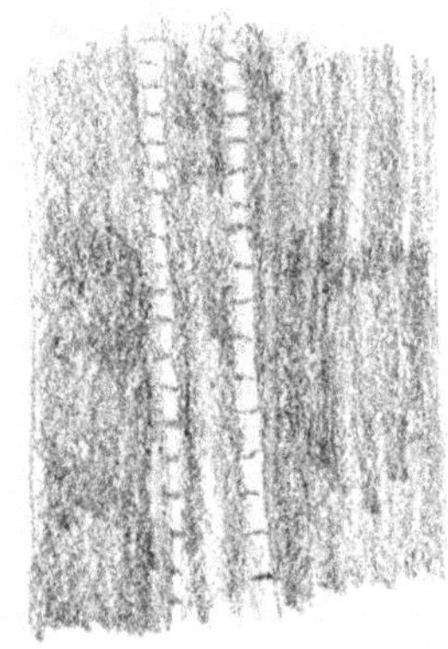

Aim

- To experience and practise relaxation activities to promote calmness and reduced tension.

Instructions

- **All**: Explain the activity to young people before doing it. Have them sit for a few minutes and notice how their clothes feel on their body. Explain that you will talk through different clothes and they can concentrate on them. Give each young person a stack of books or heavy items and they can choose a scarf or item of clothing to have in front of them. Explain that you will tell them when to put the scarf on and when to put the books on their lap. Use the script below or something similar depending on the needs of the young people and preferred language.

Example script

- Focus on your breath. Take a long slow deep breath in, hold and then breathe out. In, hold and then breathe out. Do this five more times in your own time.
- Notice what your clothes feel like on your arms. Can you feel the seams? Notice your tummy and back. Can you feel the chair/floor on your back and legs? What do your trousers/skirt/shorts etc. feel like? Are they tight or loose? Notice any creases.
- (Optional) Stand up and walk on the spot swinging your arms. Focus on the feeling that the clothes make while moving.
- Now put a scarf on or take a jumper off (with a t-shirt underneath). Does it feel different? How does it feel different? Lighter? Heavier? Tickly? Warmer/cooler?
- Now put something heavy on your lap. Focus on how this pressure feels? Calming? Irritating?
- Discuss at an appropriate level what that was like. What did they notice? What was comfortable or uncomfortable? At an introductory level go around the group asking them one thing that they noticed.

Equipment

- Different clothes to add onto your own. E.g. scarves (woollen, cotton, silk like), jumper cardigan etc.
- Heavy items e.g. books, enough for each young person.

Talking Points related to this session

- Persevering.
- Getting along with others.
- Coping with difficulties.
- Everyone is different and that's ok – learn to love yourself.
- Like vs. good at: You can like something that you are not necessarily great at.
- Managing feelings.
- Assertive, compared with passive and aggressive.
- Working towards your own life goals.
- Our actions and words/language have an impact on others.
- Getting along with others

Activity sheets for session 7

Activity	Clothes
Sport	
Party	
Sleeping	
'Lounging' at home	
At school	
At a place of worship or in the community, e.g. shops.	

Types of clothes	What does this say/mean? Possible characteristics.

Characteristics I have now	Characteristics I want/ What do I want to be like?	What do I want to do in the future? What characteristics do I need to be able to reach my goal e.g. work/college?

Session 8 Clothes from around the world

Mindfulness

Describe what others are wearing without looking

Note: Facilitators can come into group wearing different clothing from around the world. This works particularly well at engaging the young people and getting their interest. Therefore, this should be attempted wherever possible.

Aim

- To experience and practise being in the moment, focusing on the here and now.

Instructions

- **Introductory**: Describe a person's clothes while looking at them.
- **Developing**: One person covers themselves with a sheet and wraps it around themselves (head showing) and another tries to remember and describe what they are wearing. Or they could simply turn their back to that person and describe what they are wearing. Go around the group so each person has a turn. Discuss what strategies or how they remembered what others were wearing.
- **Experienced**: One person goes out of the room. All the people in the room change something about their appearance, e.g. swap watches, take something off etc. The person comes back in and is told the number of things that changed. The person then has to look closely and notice and guess what has changed. Clues can be given after some time.

AND/OR

The mindfulness activity in Session 15 'Nature', the mindfulness walk, could also be used in this session to notice things that you haven't noticed before.

Equipment

- Traditional dress from anywhere in the world

Identity

Clothes people wear around the world

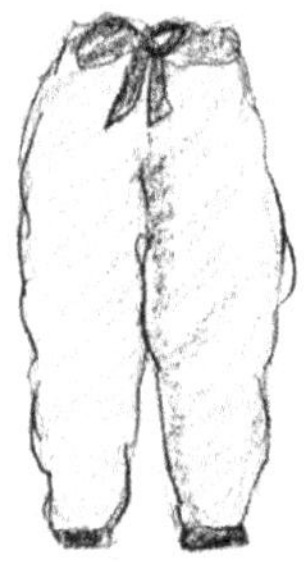

Aim

- To learn about clothes from around the world and how they are similar to and different from your own.

Instructions

- Invite the young people to bring in any traditional clothes they have from different cultures/religions as appropriate the week before. It may also be helpful to call parents/carers the week and night before to ask them if this is possible.

- Staff could also bring in different clothes.

AND/OR

- Print pictures of clothes from the different countries e.g.
    - Somalia
    - British
    - Scotland
    - Jamaica
    - India
    - Nigeria

- **Introductory**:
    - The young people could choose their favourite and try this on.
    - Describe your own favourite clothes and a time when you wore them.

- **Developing:** People from different cultures wear different clothes.
  - Look at pictures – guess where they are from. Match the country to the clothes. This could be using flags, the world map or the name of the country. The group work together to decide and match them.
  - Where are you from? What do they wear there? What do you usually wear?
- **Experienced**:
  - What does culture mean? Brainstorm.
  - Look at the clothes and match them to countries/flags around the world on the world map.
  - Why do people in different cultures wear different clothes (e.g. to keep warm, for religious reasons, because of traditions etc.)?
  - What do I wear and what does this represent, why?

The map could be used for both the food and clothes sessions and be left up on the wall for reference.

Equipment

- Clothes from different cultures
- World map
- Ribbon/string to match clothes to countries
- Pictures of clothes and names of countries they are from
- Pictures of flags

Self-esteem

The clothes I like

Aims

- Think about what clothes make you feel good in different situations. For example, favourite sports clothes or team kit help you feel confident and play well. Your favourite going out clothes help you to feel confident at a party.
- Share your own culture with others to gain a sense of confidence in who you are.

Instructions

- **Explore the following:**

What clothes do you wear? What are your favourite clothes?

Why?

How do your clothes make you feel? Comfortable? Confident? Etc.

When would you wear different clothes at different times?

- **Introductory:**

Draw your favourite clothes on your paper body.

- **Developing**: What clothes do you wear at different times (e.g. sports clothes, an apron for cooking etc.)? And why this is? What makes some clothes better for wearing at different times, e.g. light clothes for sport to keep cool or in hot weather. Use the first worksheet in Session 8 if this helps to structure the activity, which can be drawn or written as required.
- **Experienced:**
    - Worksheet: Ask each young person to complete the worksheet below. Then go around and pick out one or two each to share with the group.
    - Discussion: Use this worksheet as a basis for the discussion. Think about what clothes make you feel good in different situations, e.g. favourite sports clothes or team kit help you feel confident

and play well. Your favourite going out clothes help you to feel confident at a party. Think about what it is about these clothes that makes you feel good.

- Story: Tell a story about a time when you felt good in what you were wearing, e.g. wining a sports game in your kit, feeling confident at a party etc. Or tell a story about a 'wardrobe malfunction', i.e. an embarrassing story related to clothes. This may be too embarrassing for some young people and should not be pushed. It may be helpful for facilitators to model an embarrassing story first. The option of story should be given. This can be written as a poem or short story, or a few sentences if there is time.
- Discussion: If there are people from different cultural backgrounds in the group, similarities, differences and sharing of culture can be encouraged. If there are people from different cultural backgrounds in the group, encourage others to ask curious questions about similarities, differences and sharing of culture. This can build self-esteem as long as group members feel comfortable with this discussion.

Equipment

- Pens/pencils
- Worksheet
- Lined paper

Relaxation

Choose a fabric you like and feel it or imagine you are somewhere relaxing.

Aim

- To experience and practise relaxation activities to promote calmness and reduced tension.

Instructions

- **All**:
- Sit comfortably with your back against the floor or chair.
- Use the fabric to think of something relaxing, e.g. stroking a cat. Or focus on the sensations of the material. Maybe the fabric reminds you of something relaxing.

OR

- Choose a picture that is relaxing to you and imagine yourself being there. Place the words to guide relaxation on the table/floor so that the young people can look at these to remind/guide them what to think about and to help focus them. Does it remind you of somewhere you have been that you enjoyed and found relaxing? What can you see? What can feel? What clothes are you wearing? What can you smell? What are you doing there?

Equipment

- Different types of textured fabrics
- Relaxing images of places or things to do. Refer to the 'relaxing things' worksheet for inspiration
- Words in big print

Talking Points related to this session

- What I think may not be the whole story.
- Not knowing is ok.
- Different people have different needs.

Activity sheets for session 8

Clothes you wear?	Why?	How do I feel?
Apron	To protect my clothes when I'm cooking, in science class etc.	Safe, confident
Dress	Party. Others will be wearing similar smart clothes.	Confident, look nice, proud, happy

Words to help guide the relaxation (in big print)

See?

Hear?

Taste?

Clothes I'm wearing?

Feel?

Smell?

What am I doing?

Where am I?

Session 9 Everyday life – what do I like?

Mindfulness

Miming with an everyday object

Aim

- To experience and practise being in the moment, focusing on the here and now.

Instructions

- **All**: In this mindfulness game, have a few everyday objects, it doesn't really matter what they are, e.g. pen, ruler, piece of paper etc. Think of something else they could be and mime this. This game is about imagination and being in the moment with the rest of the group.

1 Imagine that the object is something different.

2 Mime using the object in the imaginary way (i.e. act with no sounds).

3 The rest of the group guesses what the object is.

4 The object is passed to the next person to have a go and so on.

For example, a pen could be held up beside the ear and face and used as a phone. It could be thrown against the wall like a dart etc. Pass the object round the room until each person has been given the option to mime. It may be possible to have more goes with the same object if there are more ideas. If there is time and the group are enjoying the game, use a different object to spark more imagination.

Identity

What do I like doing every day?

Aim

- To think about what you like doing every day and how that contributes to making you who you are.

Instructions

- Find pictures for a range of daily activities depicting self-care, school/college or leisure that are appropriate for your group.
- Ideas of everyday activities: waking up, washing, dressing, making breakfast, making a snack, making a drink, travelling (e.g. walk, bus, tube, taxi, train etc.), listening to instructions and doing class work, working in a group, writing, playing with friends, having a conversation, sports, talking with others, watching TV, cinema, homework, eating a meal, having a bath, going to sleep, sleeping through the night, riding a bike, sports, evening groups (e.g. youth clubs etc.)
- **Introductory**: Show pictures of daily activities (above). Ask the young people to pick out things they like or do. Stick these on individual sheets to show the things that are part of their morning afternoon and evening, i.e. creating their routine for the day or part of the day.

OR

Sequence activities that happen in the day. A facilitator can put a sequence together that doesn't make sense (which can be humorous) and the young people can correct it. Note that some won't have a 'right' order, e.g. some people brush their teeth when they get up and others before they leave the house. But you wouldn't arrive at school in your pyjamas and then put your clothes on! Have a set of pictures for part of the day, e.g. a morning routine (wake up, shower, have breakfast, get dressed, travel to school) for each young person. Ask the young people to put these in the right order, then share with the group.

- **Developing**: Show pictures of a variety of activities, including college, university and a variety of jobs. Ask the young people to pick out things they do now. Then think about what they would like to do in the future and choose some pictures for these and stick them on their paper bodies with the titles 'things I do now' and 'things I want to do in the future'. Have them go around and describe their choices, then add more details to the pictures, e.g. what they would like to study at college. If what they do or want to do is not there, they can write or draw this.

- **Experienced**: Ask the young people to call out activities they do every day and write these on a big piece of paper or the board. Go around the group and each person says or highlights with a different colour pen which ones they enjoy.

Discussion

- A discussion can be held around how different activities you enjoy every day contribute to making you the person you are. How do other people see you (e.g. organised, hardworking, funny)? How do you want to be seen?

- A collection of adjectives describing characteristics could be used so young people could pick ones that apply to them and the ones they would like to be. They can discuss how they can become more like the desired characteristics. Other young people may have ideas to help them, encourage this.

Equipment

- Pictures of different activities and different career paths

Self-esteem

What do I do every day that I'm good at?

Aim

- To feel a sense of achievement that they are good at things.

Instructions

- Give each person yellow stars to write or draw things they are good at.
- **Introductory**: On the stars, write/draw up to three things that they are good at. Use every day pictures from previous activities as a prompt if needed. They can also provide a support for drawing or writing.
- **Developing**: On the stars, write/draw three things that they are good at every day and discuss what skills are needed, e.g. football –coordination, strength, self-control, teamwork, assisting others to score, timing, thinking etc. When sharing at the end, their peers can add to the worksheet, helping individuals see even more skills they have.
- **Experienced**: On the stars (if not too basic, otherwise use squares of paper, e.g. credit card sized), write or draw three things you're good at. Discuss what skills you have and how you know you are good at it – feel you're good yourself, find it easy, other people tell you that you're good. What other skills would you like to have? How can you do more of these things? What impact will this have (e.g. make you happier, more confident etc.)?
- **All**: Compliments

Try to make sure you have enough time for the compliments, as this can be useful for many young people. Everyone write compliments on a star for the person sitting on one side based on things that they are good at, and it's better if it's not what they have already identified. This could be personal characteristics, e.g. kind when you gave me the ruler I needed or good at football etc. Try to get some context or more details from the young people when feeding back to the group and then give the star to the person, who can stick it on their body outlines. If there's time, do this again for the person on the other side.

- They can put their stars onto their body outlines to remind themselves each week of their skills.

Equipment

- Cut out of stars
- Pens and pencils

Relaxation

Sleeping activity

Aim

- To experience and practise relaxation activities to promote calmness and reduced tension.

Instructions

- Imagine you are relaxing to go to bed. Lie down and feel the floor, sit on a chair with head supported (e.g. against the wall).
- **Introductory**: Play sleeping lions – try to lie still and be quiet. Who can keep still longest?
- **Developing**: Have the young people lie down on the floor or sit in a chair with their back and head supported. Have them feel the floor/chair. The activity leader focuses on one body part at a time and reminds them to let each part of their body release (feet, legs, tummy, chest, breathing, shoulders, face – use pictures for these to reduce the language load if required). Use the relaxation script or a version of this that meets the needs of the young people as appropriate.
- **Experienced**: Have the young people find a position to sit or lie down where they feel comfortable. Have them focus on relaxing each part of their body from their feet, legs, tummy, chest, breathing, shoulders, face. Use the relaxation script or a version of this that meets the needs of the young people as appropriate.

Autogenic relaxation script

- Think about your feet. Feel the floor underneath your feet. Imagine them becoming warm.
- Think about your calves. Feel them resting on the floor as they feel heavy. Imagine them becoming warm.
- Focus your knees. Feel the warmth of relaxation flow up through your knees into your thighs.
- Focus on your tummy rising and falling as you breathe slowly in and out. Imagine your tummy becoming warm.
- Feel your back against the chair or floor and the places where it meets the floor. Is there tension in your back? As you breathe out, imagine the tension drifting away and the warmth of relaxation.

- Focus on your hands, your fingers, the palms of your hands. Relax your hands and feel the warmth flow into your hands.
- Think about your forearms. Think about your upper arms and shoulders. Relax them onto the floor further as they become warm. Feel the floor or chair underneath.
- Think about your face. Relax the muscles in your forehead, around your eyes, cheeks and jaw. As you relax your muscles, feel them become warmer and the tension go.
- Feel your whole body being heavy and sinking a little. If you feel an area of tension, focus on this and releasing that tension, feeling the warmth of relaxation.
- Now enjoy this feeling of being warm and relaxed and heavy for a few moments.

Equipment

- Space is needed
- Exercise/Yoga mats or high back chair
- Autogenic relaxation script

Talking Points related to this session

- We aren't all good at everything.
- Not knowing is ok.
- Coping with difficulties.
- Everyone is different and that's ok – learn to love yourself.
- Like vs. good at: You can like something that you are not necessarily great at.
- Managing feelings.
- Promote healthy lifestyles.

Activity sheets for session 9

Stars of things I am good at

Things I do everyday

Morning	Afternoon	Evening

Session 10 Sport and exercise – what do I like? My teams and games

Mindfulness

Complete a maze

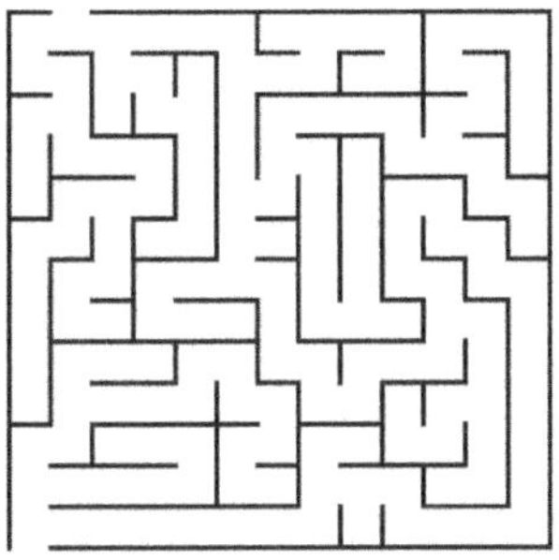

Aim

- To experience and practise being in the moment, focusing on the here and now.

Instructions

- Pick the maze or the young people choose the maze that they want to draw.
- Focus on tracing through the maze for the allocated time. You could carry on with another one if you finish before the time.
- Reflect and share and share experiences in the group.
- Focus again.

Equipment

- Three different levels of difficulty of mazes (download these from the internet)

Identity

Sports personalities

Aim

- To think about different sports personalities (hearing and d/Deaf) and what they are known for.
- What sport teams/people do I like?

Instructions

- If there is a particular sporting event around the time you are doing this, e.g. Olympics, football world cup or athletics championships etc., this can be incorporated into the group and used as an example. Clips of sports or sports people could be shown, e.g. from the internet and discussed if resources allow.
- **Introductory**: Go around the group and try to name a sport you know for each letter of the alphabet. This can be quite open and extend to things related to sports, as being involved is the aim not assessing their knowledge of sport! A facilitator could write these on a big sheet of paper or board if useful. If some letters are blank, this is ok, it doesn't have to be perfect; everyone in the group is trying their best.

  AND/OR

  Write on the paper bodies your favourite sports, teams or sports people. Try to encourage understanding of each other and differences and tolerance of others, e.g. different football teams that are liked. Avoid arguments in this area by facilitating discussions and encouraging the group to listen to everyone's point of view and accepting this, rather than someone insisting that their team is best. Be prepared with how to manage this if you know it might be an issue for the young people.

- **Developing**: Look at pictures and recognise who they are. The group can put them in order of how famous they are, requiring negation skills. This could be done in two groups with different famous sports people and then summarised for the other half when they have finished. Discuss why they are known, e.g. for shouting or getting in trouble, being the best, or married to someone famous etc. Staff to have information about them but accept that the group may not know some information. Write on paper bodies who their favourite team/sport etc. is.
- **Experienced**: Name different sports personalities and explain to group why they are famous. What is your favourite team, why? Link identity to having a team and being part of their supporters. What does this mean?

Note: Many famous people have difficulties with things. Some famous people have other diagnoses, e.g. dyslexia, mental health difficulties (depression, anxiety etc.), or may feel they are not good enough in other areas of their lives. If you feel this is going to be a useful discussion for your young people, take some time to research famous people and famous sports people with difficulties and use these stories in discussions.

Equipment

- Pictures of various sports, sports teams and sports personalities

Self-esteem

Make a sport equipment outline and write/draw personal strengths in this

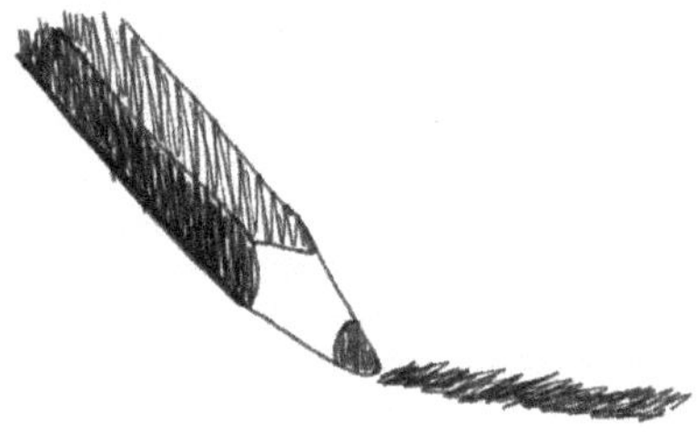

Aim

- To identify sport and exercise strengths (skills and likes).

Instructions

- **Introductory**: Have the young people draw the outline of a piece of sports or gym equipment that they like and record their skills in this, which can then be stuck on their body outline. Adult-led identification of strengths will be used more at this level, or depending on the skill and age of group members, they can choose skills from the 'Sports skills' list in Session 10.
- **Developing**: Choose pictures of sport equipment and write personal strengths and likes around/on these. Participants identify their own strengths or sports they like with additions by adults if needed.
- **Experienced**: Discuss strengths and support young people to identify their own strengths and those of others.

Equipment

- Paper
- Cardboard
- Stapler (with care)
- Scissors (with care)
- Pencils/pens

Relaxation

Moving in rhythm with your breathing

Aim

- To experience and practise relaxation activities to promote calmness and reduced tension.

Instructions

- **All**: Breathe in and make a movement and breathe out and make another movement. For example, breathe in and raise your arms above your head, breathe out while bending over and touching your toes. Below are some ideas of different complexities for the different levels. Come up with your own ideas to lead the group with. Remember all of these movements should be slow and controlled in time with deep slow breaths to aid relaxation.

  Repeat this 5–10 times. This could also be done in rhythm with some relaxing music. See the 'Relaxation instructions' in Sessions 10 for some ideas.

- **Introductory**: See the 'Relaxation instructions' in Session 10 for other ideas at this level.

- **Developing and Experienced:**

  - Create more complex movements for those who are able to manage this. They could also include two movements at the same time. A balance aspect could also be added. See 'Relaxation instructions' in Session 10 for ideas at this level.

  - Once the young people get the idea, they can come up with their own ideas and the group can follow these.

Note: make sure all the movements are safe for everyone and that you have a safe environment with sufficient room for everyone to move without hitting each other or any objects.

Talking Points related to this session

- We aren't all good at everything.

- Managing difficulties in life.

- Promote healthy lifestyles.
- Working towards your own life goals.
- What I think may not be the whole story.
- Everyone is different and that's ok – learn to love yourself.
- Like vs. good at: You can like something that you are not necessarily great at.
- Managing feelings.

Activity sheets for session 10

Sports skills

- Being fit
- Running fast
- Running a long distance
- Strong
- Flexible
- Getting along with others
- Working as a team for the team to win
- Passing so someone else can score for the team
- Following instructions from the coach
- Concentrating and having good focus
- Confident in your skills
- Continuing even if you don't win
- Coping with making a mistake (e.g. missing a shot)
- Having fun playing sport
- Being supportive to others if they miss a shot, not blaming or getting angry with them
- Working with others even if you disagree with them
- Trying your hardest
- Following the rules
- Being disciplined
- Practising as well as playing games

Relaxation instructions

Introductory

Breathe in	Breathe out
Raise arms straight above your head straight out in front of you	Lower arms to your sides
Raise arms straight above your head to the sides	Lower arms to your sides
Raise arms out to the side and stretch	Lower arms to your sides
With feet on the floor, slowly twist body round to one side, breathe out and come back to the centre slowly. Breathe in and slowly twist to the opposite side.	Come back to the centre slowly
Bending your arms at the elbow with palms up, bring your hands in front of your face	Lower your arms back to your sides
Starting with both hands on one side of your hip/leg, breathe in and raise both hands at your side together over your head stop at the top	Lower both arms together to hands on the opposite leg/hip (do the same on the other side)
Step one leg out to the side	Step back so your feet are together. Repeat on the other side.
Step one leg in front	Step back so your feet are together. Repeat on the other side.
Step one leg behind you	Step back so your feet are together. Repeat on the other side.

Developing and Experienced

Breathe in	Breathe out
Stretch up on your tip toes with arms above your head	Touch your toes and crouch down
Stretch your arms out to the side while stepping one leg out to the side	Step your leg in and lower your arms down. Do the same on the other side.
Circle both arms together behind your back and over your head	Lower them down in front of you. Do this in the opposite direction.
Step forward with one leg, raising the opposite hand in front of you and the other one behind	Step back with feet together and lower arms. Do the same on the other side.
Lift one leg out to the side while balancing on the other. You could raise both arms out to the side. This could also be done in front and behind	Lower your legs and arms down. Do the same on the other side.
Bend forward at the hip raising one leg out behind you, reaching forward with opposite hand.	Lower leg and arm to a standing position. Do the same on the other side.

Session 11 Exercise – my body and relaxation

Mindfulness

Thinking about my muscles

Aim

- To experience and practise being in the moment, focusing on the here and now.

Instructions

- Tell the young people that we have muscles all over our bodies. Ask them to find one in a leg, hand, arm or foot and watch it work. How does it feel?
- **Introductory**: Invite the young people to choose a muscle on themselves. Practise focusing on it together.
- **Developing**: Identify muscles that each person will focus on as a group, take time to focus and reflect. Then choose which muscle to focus on next.
- **Experienced**: Individuals select their own focus, try to focus on the muscle, reflect and focus again. Discuss situations when this activity could be used outside the group.

Identity

What do I do to help my body relax?

Aim

- Identifying activities that relax each person.

Instructions

- Different people find different things relaxing. It is important to regularly (every day) do things that are relaxing and fun to help us feel calmer more of the time.
- **Introductory**: Young people and facilitators go around and pick a card from a pack of relaxing ideas and one by one mime them. The others have to guess what they are doing. There could be a quick discussion after each, asking if anyone finds that activity relaxing or not. They could stand by a 'relaxing' sign or a 'not relaxing' sign on either side of the room after each to make the activity more interesting. Ideas of relaxing activities for children: bath, blowing bubbles, laughing, singing, running around, sport, cuddle, listening to a story etc. Have them draw one thing on their paper body that is relaxing.
- **Developing**: Briefly explain that relaxation and tension are the opposite of each other. Go around and create a list on the board of activities that are relaxing and those that create tension. They could be dancing, arguing, being told off, disagreeing with someone, being upset, bath, cuddle, losing game, playing a team game, failing, succeeding, speaking in assembly etc. (see the list 'Do these create tension or help you relax?' in the resources section below). There could be multiple layers to these, e.g. if you're losing a game it may create tension but if you're winning you might feel more relaxed. This could stimulate some discussion. Remind the young people there is no right and wrong and different people find different things relaxing.
- **Experienced**: The young people take some time to write down the things they find relaxing and those that cause them tension (see 'Do these create tension or help you relax?' list below). Then have them remember a time when they felt tense and what happened to help them feel relaxed/calm again (use activity sheet if helpful) and go around and share their stories. Facilitators should elicit the things that helped them relax and deal with the difficult situation. Write on paper bodies or folder the skills that the young people have to relax in the face of difficulty.

  Describe the stressful event. How did you feel? What were you thinking? What happened next and what did you do? How did you feel calm/relaxed again?

Self-esteem

I like my body. I've got good. . . . My body is good at. . . .

strength, coordination, timing (clapping to the beat of music), eye-hand coordination (flick a table tennis ball into a small goal).

Aim

- To identify abilities your body is good at.

Instructions

- Discuss different aspects of physical skill, name body parts (for younger members try all the above skills – which are we each good at?).
- **Introductory**:
  - Use a body outline (not one of the young people's) to name different body parts. These could be labelled. If private parts are named, either use words everyone is comfortable with or try to refocus on body parts that are used for exercise or relaxation. If this is not appropriate, acknowledge the response and refocus on parts that are used for exercise. Use whatever language is appropriate for the young people and setting.

  The young people then take part in these activities

  - Speed – Time running from one side of the playground/hall to the other.
  - Balance – Who can balance on one foot for longest (timed)?
  - Stretch – How far can you reach when bending over (e.g. touch your toes, shins, ankles without bending your knees)?
  - Rhythm – Clap in time with music, then make up some rhythms to match the music.
  - Eye-hand coordination (e.g. throw a table tennis ball/beanbag into a small goal/bucket).
  - Name skills related to body parts and add them to the body outline (e.g. arms – strong or using a racket; legs – running fast, rhythm and dancing; muscles – strong; tummy – core strength and balance). If young people are having difficulty understanding this, use sports that these body parts are needed for.

- Go around the group and encourage each young person to identify which ability they use and when they use it and what they are good at.

- **Developing**:
  - List the skills above and cut out on cards. Put these face down in a container. Each person picks a card and thinks about what that ability is needed for the activity, e.g. balance for gymnastics. Go around the group one by one and share with the group.
  - Put the ability cards face up in the middle of the table/floor, invite the young people to draw the ability on your paper body that you are good and what it helps with, e.g. a sport or interest (this may be linked to likes or skills thought about in previous groups, for example, I'm good with my hands as I have neat handwriting). Or, have extra pictures that can be stuck on paper bodies.

- **Experienced: discussion questions**
  - What do you do to relax?
  - How often?
  - Encourage use of relaxation at home throughout the week at the end of the session before. Check out how this went the week after doing more relaxation. What did they do? When? How often? Useful or not?
  - Does relaxation make you feel different?
  - What happens when you do more?
  - What happens when you don't relax?
  - Impact of stress and relaxation. When you are stressed what happens to your body? Thoughts? And temperament? Think of a time when you have felt stressed – What happened? How did you react? What helped you feel more relaxed?
  - On the board have two outlines of a person – one tense and one relaxed. Have each young person come up and draw/write something that happens to a body when it is relaxed on one body outline and when it is tense on the other. Discuss these.
  - Choose a relaxation strategy to use in a stressful situation in the coming week. Remember next week to check in on how it went during the intro or relaxation activity at the end.

Equipment

- Words and pictures for different body parts and skills

Relaxation

Balance or progressive muscle relaxation

Aims

- Concentrate on balancing and breathing.
- Notice the difference between tension and relaxation in our bodies.

Instructions

- Find a comfortable way to stand and balance with your eyes shut.
- Balance and think about your breathing when the group leader touches your arm.
- Stop balancing when the group leader touches you again on the arm or says stop.

Talking points related to this session

- Relaxation
    - Psycho-educational concerning exercise link to self-esteem and feeling good (e.g. mood).
    - A time when they enjoyed exercise/sport (role play or describing).
    - Help the young person identify what they liked about it, why it was so good.
    - Draw or write a short description (to stick on paper bodies if time and if appropriate).
    - Encourage exercise/sport often, e.g. five vigorous 30-minute times a week.
- Promoting healthy lifestyles
    - Discuss that the more things we do to help us feel relaxed day to day help us to deal with stress and return to feeling calm faster after difficult situations (see the 'Promoting healthy lifestyles' talking point for more details).
- Different people have different needs – what suits one person may not suit another person.

Activity sheets for session 11

What helps you relax?

Having a bath	Going for a walk
Blowing bubbles	Having your hair brushed
Singing	Having a shower
Running	Sitting in the garden
Playing sport	Having a cuddle
Listening to a story	Listening to music
Swimming	Going to bed
Thinking of others	

Put ideas on cards for young people to hold up to express their opinion. These could be cut out and stuck to ice lolly sticks or a pencil.

RELAXING	NOT RELAXING

Do these create tension or help you relax?

Dancing	Arguing	Succeeding
Being told off	Being upset	Speaking in assembly
Disagreeing with someone	Losing a game	Having a bath
Playing computer games	Playing a team game	Singing
Being on your phone	Failing	Sitting in the garden
Going for a walk	Having your hair brushed	Having a shower
Blowing bubbles	Having a cuddle	Gardening
Running	Listening to music	Swimming
Playing sport	Going to bed	Listening to a story

Feeling relaxed or tense

Situations that make me relaxed	Situations that make me tense

How I can relax

Situations where I feel tense Write the who, what, where here	How I feel more relaxed. Discuss things you have tried or ideas from the group for each situation.

Session 12 My body – growing and changing

Mindfulness

Watching a clock

Aim

- To experience and practise being in the moment, focusing on the here and now.

Instructions

- Encourage the young people to watch the clock.
- Think about the 'present moment' or 'now'.
- If your mind wanders to the past or future, bring it back to now.
- Reflect and discuss briefly.
- Watch the clock again.

Identity

Create your own timeline

Baby child teenager adult older person

I_______I__________I___________I__________I_____________I

Aims

- To discuss life stages and the young people's understanding of their roles at each stage.
- Create your own timeline.

Instructions

- Draw or gather pictures of people at different life stages – create a timeline for each participant. Mark where that child or young person is now on the timeline from baby to older person.
- **Introductory**:
    - Create a group timeline. Cut out and stick pictures of different aged people on the timeline. Young people could pick one and go around sticking it to the timeline.
    - "In the future I want to be . . .": Draw or go around and explain what you want to be when you're an adult, e.g. job, family etc. Write/draw these on your paper bodies.
- **Developing**:
    - Everyone draws their own timeline (or use worksheet) and writes or draws what they enjoyed doing at different ages in the past, or the good things about being that age. Then go around and share this with the group.
    - What are you future hopes? Write/draw these on the timeline when they would happen. These can be discussed or simply shared.
- **Experienced: Discuss places, people and roles for each stage of life – memories and hopes**
    - Use the timeline template and write memories from different times in your life. Go around and share these with the group.
    - Write ideas and plans for the future, e.g. when married/children, what career or study do you want to do, etc. Where will you be living and who with at different times? Will you travel?

Self-esteem

What do I like about my body? (What is my favourite age and why?)

Aims

- To identity parts of your body that you like.
- To discuss benefits of different stages of life.

Instructions

- There are two parts to this section: (1) What do I like about my body? and (2) What is my favourite age? Feel free to do one or the other or both, depending on which matches the needs of the group and time.
- **Introduction**:
    - Part 1: Which of my body parts do I like? Stick arrows on paper bodies showing parts you like. This could be linked to things you like doing, e.g. I like my legs because they help me play football.
    - Part 2: Use photos of participants or people at different stages of life from magazines/newspapers etc. Each young person chooses a picture and gives an idea about why it's good to be at school, at work, a baby, elderly. Pictures can be chosen or taken from a pile face down or chosen from looking through magazines/newspapers. The facilitator can provide a forced alternative suggestion, e.g. Is being a baby good because you can sleep a lot or because you are learning to crawl? This could be done a second time with everyone taking a different age picture and saying something different about that age.
- **Developing**:
    - Part 1: Which of my body parts do I like? Stick arrows on paper bodies showing parts you like and reasons why. This could be linked to things you like doing, e.g. I like my legs because they help me play football.
    - As a group, participants identify something positive about each age. This could be a list on the board. Pictures could be used to prompt ideas.

- **Experienced:**
  - Discussion around body parts individuals like and don't like. Discuss how this is linked to feeling good about yourself or not. If appropriate, parts they don't like could be shared and facilitated carefully in order that the young people leave feeling more positive about their bodies. Identify favourite body parts on their paper bodies, which could be recorded with an arrow or any way they like.
  - Discuss body image: the value we have about our image. The media's role in image could be discussed.
  - Using their timeline, each participant identifies something that is positive about each age. Discussion and reflection on people they know is facilitated to support this process.

Note: In discussions about age, differences in bodies can be discussed as appropriate to the group.

Relaxation

Being small and getting bigger

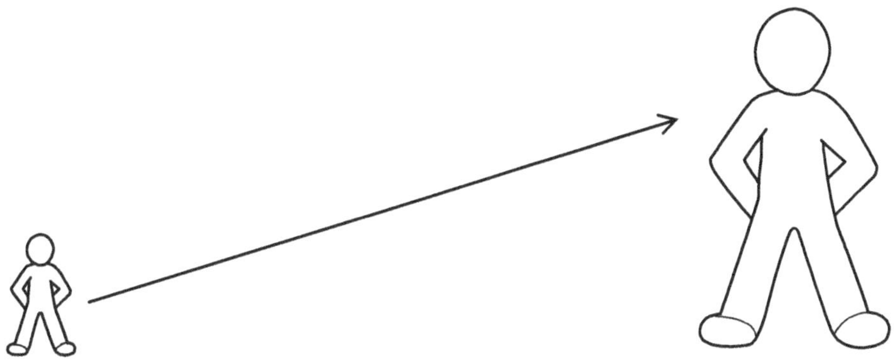

Aim

- Tense: tall and straight; Relaxed – small and floppy.

Instructions

- **Introduction**: Invite the young people to stand upright, as tall as they can stretching their arms up. Then flop down and become small.
- **Developing**: Do the above but introduce more graded sizes. Discuss where they are tense/tight and where they are loose/floppy.
- **Experienced**: Do the above and ask the participants to introduce their own ideas, related to different ages and sizes and to take the lead. Notice the difference in body movements and how this can help to relax.

Equipment

- Pictures of different aged people they can use for inspiration and stick on worksheet

Talking points related to this session

- Persevering.
    - Sometimes you need to try relaxation activities several times before they help you relax.
- Getting along with others.

Activity sheets for session 12

Timeline sheet

Baby	child	teenager	adult	older person

Me				
Other people				

Growing and changing

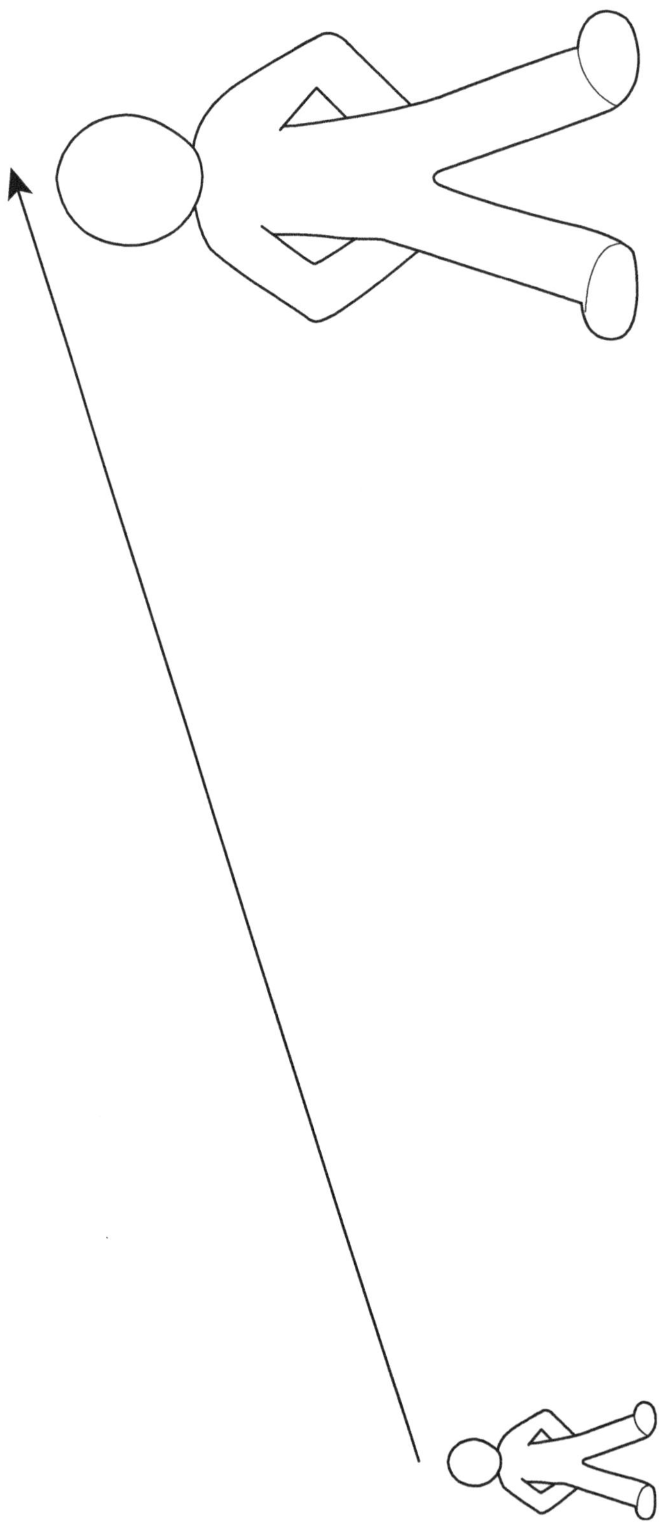

Session 13 Gender – my body and stereotypes

Mindfulness

Focus on a body part

Aim

- To experience and practise being in the moment, focusing on the here and now.

Instructions

- **All**:
    - Look at a part of your body, e.g. hand or forearm. What do you notice? How does it feel? Is it resting on something? What does this feel like?
    - Reflect.
    - Focus again.
- **Intro**: Go around the group and say one thing that you noticed.
- **Developing**: Go around the group and say two things that you noticed and how well you felt that you focused.
- **Experienced**: Discuss young people's experiences and then mindfulness in general. You could use the following discussion points:
    - Do you feel mindfulness is becoming easier?
    - How are you experiencing the increase in length of time?
    - Is it useful?
    - Can you use it at different times?
    - For a bit of psycho-education around the benefits of mindfulness in everyday life, see Chapter 2.

Identity

What does gender mean to me?

Looking after babies?

Fighting fires?

Aim

- To identify what being a boy/man, girl/woman means to each person and discuss stereotypes.

Instructions

- There are many ideas for activities within this section. Please choose the ones that are most appropriate for the group. It is not expected all these would occur in a single group.
- **Expectations of being a boy or girl**: Linked with gender, think about ways in which people are stereotyped due to gender (e.g. if you are a boy you *should* . . . , if you are a girl you *should* . . .)
    - Body (men strong, women weak, genitals)
    - Clothes/accessories
    - Jobs
    - Characteristics (women mild, quiet, men strong)
    - Money earned
    - Hairstyles
    - Jobs/chores at home
- **Characteristics of being a boy/girl**: Think about the characteristics of being a boy or a girl. Brainstorm on the paper with these on either side:
    - All girls are. . . (bad at science, quiet, good readers, girly, fussy, tidy, can't throw etc.)
    - All boys are. . . (loud, boisterous, annoying, good at maths, good at sport, smelly etc.)

- Think of famous people who defy these stereotypes. This will need to be researched prior to the group and pictures printed.
- Then tear this up/rub it off the board at the end and throw it away as a symbol that it doesn't matter. And of wanting to treat all people as individuals, supporting their individual identity.
- Developing: What did you want to be when you were younger (career)? Are these linked with gender stereotypes? Has this changed over time? Do you want to be something different now?

- **Experienced:**
    - There are actual differences between male and female bodies, e.g. men are generally stronger but some women are stronger than most men – female weight lifters; women often have slimmer bodies but there are exceptions, e.g. Mo Farah.
    - Yes, there are differences between men and women, but should this have an impact on how we treat others or the choices that we make for ourselves?
    - Gender stereotypes exist in culture and media and we can't avoid them. But we can treat others with respect of their decisions and diversity, and we can have the courage to be who we want to be even though others may not agree or like it. It's also ok to be a feminine girl or masculine boy and be what others may feel is stereotypical. Some aspects might be stereotypical and other aspects not, e.g. a girl who wants to be a nurse but also loves playing football. Have the group try to think of one thing that is typical for their gender and one thing that is not typical. Have they been treated any different in terms of these things?
    - Complete a sheet of positives and challenges of being male or female with the group.
    - How you dress? Which music do you listen to? Does this mean a certain thing? For example, if you listen to rap and wear similar clothes, what will others think if they saw you on the street? Is this a fair judgement?
- **Discussion topics/questions:**
    - What are the effects on others of stereotyping? For example, sad, can't be themselves, lack of identity, lack of confidence.
    - Can you think of times when people have discriminated against you? If you want to, describe the situation. How did you feel? How did you manage this? What did you learn from this?
    - What does it mean to be male or female?
    - What makes you male or female?
    - What does this enable you to do? What does it stop you from doing?
    - Is stereotyping helpful?

- Have you experienced times when this has been helpful or constricting?
- How can we be open minded to respect other people's identity? Ideas: not assuming someone is straight, e.g. asking about their partner rather than using a gender.

Note: Sexual orientation may come up here. Decide before how you want to go about discussing this in an open, accepting way.

Equipment

- Worksheet for discussion of traditional male or female jobs, roles and skills
- Photos/resources of people that break these stereotypes
- Man/woman worksheet
- Pictures of relevant famous people.
- Pictures and words for activities, jobs and roles
- Weight-lifting women
- Women doctors
- Male midwives
- Women footballers
- Celebrities – Boy George

Self-esteem

I like being a boy/girl because. . .

Boy? Girl?

Aim

- To discuss gender.

Instructions

- **All**: Begin exploring what being a girl or boy means for the participants. This is their view about what they like about their gender. (Their ideas may not match the facilitator's view, which may need further discussion in reflection and planning with other facilitators.)
- **Intro**: Draw on their paper bodies something they like about being a boy/girl, e.g. skirt, football boots.
- **Developing**: Think of several ideas about what they like, share with the group and encourage listening.
- **Experienced**: Explore what each participant likes about their gender. Is this the same for other members of their family of the same or different genders?

Relaxation

Breathing

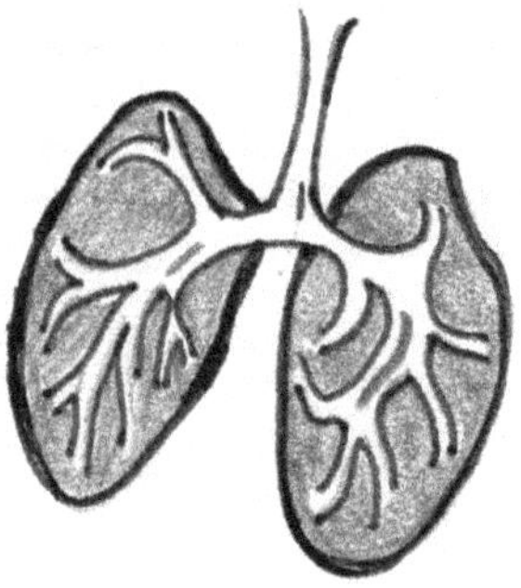

Aim

- To introduce relaxation activities.
- Recap and explain relaxation – relaxing your body and mind, learning to feel peaceful.
- Discuss breathing and try focusing on this for one minute.

Instructions

- Explain that activities will focus on different parts of the body and will last different lengths of time. Different people like different ways to relax. We hope everyone can find something they like.

Equipment

- Comfortable seating

Talking points related to this session

- Everyone is different and that's ok – learn to love yourself.
    - If this is an identified talking point for your group, take the opportunity to explore how we are each different from what's 'expected', when we notice being different and how we might feel about that.
- Our actions and language have an impact on others.
- Managing difficulties in life – if you want to do something people don't expect or want you to do.

Activity sheets for session 13

Jobs, skills and roles

People expect women to be. . .	People expect men to be. . .
People don't expect women to be. . .	**People don't expect men to be. . .**

Identity and gender – positives and challenges

Positives

Positives

Challenges

Boy?

Girl?

Challenges

Session 14 Relationships and my family

Mindfulness

Favourite person

Aim

- To experience and practise being in the moment, focusing on the here and now.

Instructions

- **All**: Think about your favourite person or someone you like and how you feel when you are with them.
  - Focus
  - Reflect
  - Focus again
- **Introduction**: Use a photo of a family member or friend for the young person to focus on.
- **Developing**: Draw the person and then use this picture of the person you have drawn.
- **Experienced**: Imagine the feelings.

Equipment

- Photos and pictures

Identity

Who am I for other people (roles and responsibilities)?

Sister? Brother? Pupil? Friend? Helper? Cook? Footballer?

Aim

- To think about who you are through other people's eyes

Instructions

- Think about different topics such as
  - Family tree
  - Relationship titles
  - How you help them
  - How they help you
  - What you mean to other people
  - How they would describe you
- **Introductory**: Have the young people draw one or two other people who are important to them on a sheet. How do they see them, as helpful, funny, a cousin, a playmate? Draw the young person – what would the other people say about them?

OR

Use photos supplied by the family to create a family tree. Allow them to tell others who the family members are.

- **Developing**: Draw yourself in the middle of a big piece of paper or write your name. Then write/draw the people that you feel are closest to you and their relation to you (friend, brother, teacher etc.). The closer a person is on the paper the closer they are in real life. Then go around and share one or two things about some of the people you have drawn. Discuss how important you are for them and what they would say about you. How would they describe you? Different people may describe you in different ways. Is there someone else who would have a different opinion?

  OR

  Draw a family tree and think about what their titles are in relation to you and who you are to them (e.g. son, cousin, grandson etc.). Discuss how important you are to them and they are to you. How would they describe you? Different people may describe you in different ways. Is there someone else who would have a different opinion?

- **Experienced**: Draw a family tree and think about what their title is in relation to other family members (e.g. son, cousin, grandson etc.). Who are you to them? This can be extended to qualities these family members may see the most, e.g. hard working, lazy, chilled out, busy. Think about the roles these people have in your life and how close this makes them to you. For example, I can talk to them, I can go to their house when I'm feeling down, they make me happy as they're fun to be around, they look after me and cook, we play football etc.

Equipment

- Pen/pencils
- Glue
- Scissors
- Paper

Self-esteem

Who am I? Personal qualities

Aim

- To encourage the group to think about their personal qualities.

Instructions

- Depending on the skill level of group members, have pictures or words prepared that represent different personal qualities or characteristics.
- **Intro**: Have the young people look at the pictures or words that represent qualities or characteristics and pick out three that describe them.
- **Developing**: Use words or pictures or both of characteristics or qualities and think about the meanings as a group. Each young person can circle the ones that describe them. Then they can write/draw or cut them out and stick them on their paper bodies.
- **Experienced**: Discuss why some people do not have certain qualities. Discuss what qualities they would like to have. What qualities do they have? Everyone tells a story about someone else in the room demonstrating when they have showed certain characteristics. Write characteristics on paper body.

Equipment

- Pictures/word cards
- Pencils/pens
- Paper/worksheet

Relaxation

Thinking about your partner's breathing

Aim

- To focus on your own and one other person's breathing.

Instructions

- Work with a partner within the group. Depending on the young people, this may be sitting apart and watching each other. If it is appropriate and group members can manage to sit back to back, they can focus on the feel of breathing from their partner.
- **Introductory**: Take it in turns for each pair to watch each other's breathing. Can they control and match their breathing when the rest of the group supports them – 'breathe in, breathe out'?
- **Developing**: As with the introductory activity but each pair takes responsibility for prompting their breathing.
- **Experienced**: Have each young person focus on the feel or look of their partner's breathing. Can they slow and match their breathing just through looking or feeling?

Talking points related to this session

- Identity.
- We aren't all good at everything.

Activity sheets for session 14

Who am I? What are my skills and qualities?

Kind, mean, caring, honest, dishonest, lovely, rude, supportive, rude, unhelpful, helpful, thoughtful, thoughtless, short in responses, harsh, friendly, welcoming, bold, argumentative, passive, placid, easy going, calm, tense, anxious, good communicator, ambitious, assertive, aggressive, happy, enthusiastic, decisive.

Think of your own words to suit your group.

What am I like?

Kind	Funny	Risk taker	Bossy
Creative	Serious	Happy	Flexible
Patient	Impatient	Angry	Aggressive
Snappy	Friendly	Calm	Shy
Caring	Anxious	Clever	Sporty
Assertive	Artistic	Impulsive	
Passive			

Session 15 Nature

Mindfulness

Being outside and noticing things in the environment.

Aim

- To experience and practise being in the moment, focusing on the here and now.

Instructions

- **Intro**: Walk outside. Collect things from nature, e.g. a leaf, stick, seed etc. Draw these or sit quietly exploring your objects.
- **Developing**: Walk outside quietly with minimal talking. Notice things that you hadn't noticed before.
- **Experienced**: Walk outside with no talking or communicating. After the walk, sit in a group and go around so the young people have an opportunity to share their experiences, what they noticed etc.

  OR

- **All**: Have some objects from nature e.g. pine cone, seeds, leaf, twigs etc.

  Hold one of the objects in your hand, feeling it and observing it. Practise being in the moment and experiencing it. Note what thoughts you might have and then bring your attention back to the experience and sensations of your nature object.

Equipment

- Things from nature, e.g. leaves, cones, seeds, twigs, grass etc.

Identity

What animal would I be?

Aim

- Think about your characteristics through choosing an animal.

Instructions

- "If you could be an animal for the day, what would you be?"
- What animal do you have similar characteristics to? Describe why you would be that animal and its similarities to you.
- **Intro**: Have pictures of animals printed, several of each. Ask the young people to pick their favourite animal that they would like to be for the day.
    - Draw or copy or trace or cut out the animal.

  OR

    - Do you have pets? What pets do you have? Draw/cut out these animals and stick them to your paper body.
    - Go around and share your work. Prompts for questions:
    - Name of pet. What do you like about your pet?
    - What would you be doing as that animal?
    - Why did you pick that animal?

- **Developing**: Draw or cut out your animal or pet. Write the characteristics that you have in common with that animal and stick this to your large paper body (e.g. lion – brave and strong; dolphin – wise and free). Go around and share these with the group.

- **Experienced**: Have the young people choose what animal they would be that matches their personality and characteristics. Discuss in the group or go around explaining why they are using those characteristics. Explore in more detail why they picked that animal and the characteristics that the young person shares with the animal.

Equipment

- Print out of animal pictures.

- Pens

- Paper

- Scissors

Self-esteem

Leading games

Aim

- To give each young person a chance to lead a small quick game to increase skills and confidence

Instructions

- **Intro**: Choose a game that has a leader, e.g. Simon Says, Captain's Coming etc. Invite all the young people to take turns in leading this game for a couple of minutes – teaching everyone as if they don't know the game. Give the least amount of support to individual young people that is required, letting them do as much as they can on their own.
- **Developing**: Choose a short game they would like to lead and support them in giving instructions if needed.
- **Experienced**: Choose a game/activity they would play. Explain it to the rest of the group and how to play it. Work with the young person to think about ways to deliver the instructions.

Note: Depending on your group size, you may need to do this over two or more weeks so everyone has a chance to lead.

Equipment

- Games ideas – statues, Simon Says, Captain's Coming, Grandmother's Footsteps, games played in your setting, games young people play at home, games from leader's childhood
- Outdoor space or indoor space (depending on game/season/space etc.)

Relaxation

Growth

Aim

- To think about growing from a seed to a tall oak tree

Instructions

- **Introductory**: Imagine that you have an acorn in your hand (or use a real one) or show a picture of an acorn
- **Developing:** As above, and then tell the story of the life cycle of the acorn – an acorn, then roots, then a shoot, then buds and leaves, then a little tree, then a big oak tree. Eventually, it drops an acorn. . .
- **Experienced:** As above, and then
    - Think about what the acorn needs to grow and change.
    - Think about what the tree needs to stay big and strong.
    - Think about sitting under the big oak tree – what can you smell, see, feel?

Equipment

- An acorn/picture of an acorn
- Life cycle of the acorn (visual cue)

Talking points related to this session

- Making mistakes and trying again.
    - Games are a great way to learn to understand and be with other people. If you make a mistake, start the game again.

Session 16 Places

Mindfulness

The room

Aim

- To experience and practise being in the moment, focusing on the here and now.

Instructions

- Focus on something in the room. Look at this and focus on the present.
- **Introduction**: Select two or three objects that are regularly in the room. Ensure these can be held. Each young person picks the object they want to use. Focus on the object for the mindfulness time.
- **Developing**: Select a small group of objects that are in the room and suggest these to the young people, with photo prompts if needed.
- **Experienced**: Ask each young person to focus on something in the room. Discuss after the first three minutes what they selected and whether they will try focusing on something different or the same for the second time.

Identity

Where do you come from?

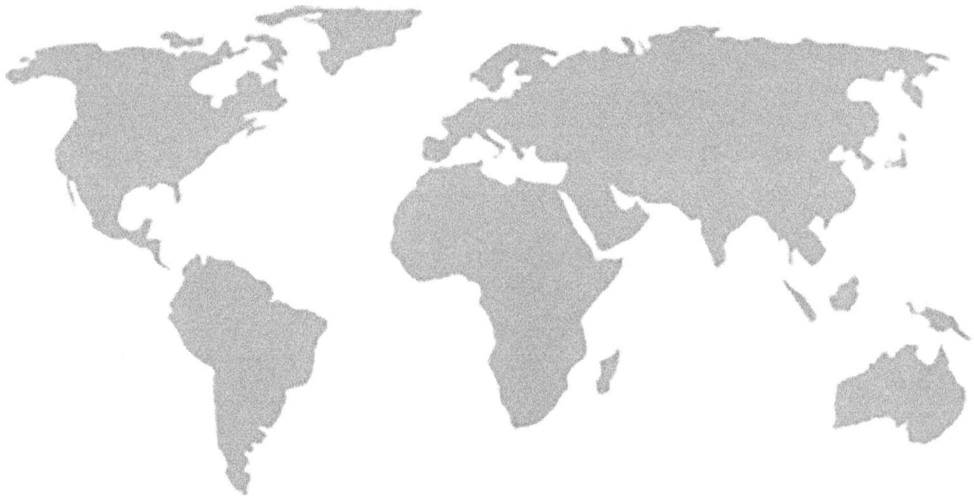

Aim

- To think about where you come from.

Instructions

- Thinking about parental relationships.
- The place where you were born.
- Where you grew up.
    - **Introduction**: Find on a map where you live. Write your address down.
    - **Developing**: Find on a map where you come from, where you were born, different areas you have lived in.
    - **Experienced**: Go around to discuss how important knowing where you come from is to identity.
- Draw/trace the country where you were born and where you have lived (if different). Stick these to your paper bodies.
- Write your name on a piece of paper and with a string link it to places you have lived on the world or UK map.

Equipment

- Maps of UK/Europe/world, depending on backgrounds of group participants
- Pens/pencils
- Paper

Self-esteem

Places that make me feel comfortable, places that make me feel uncomfortable

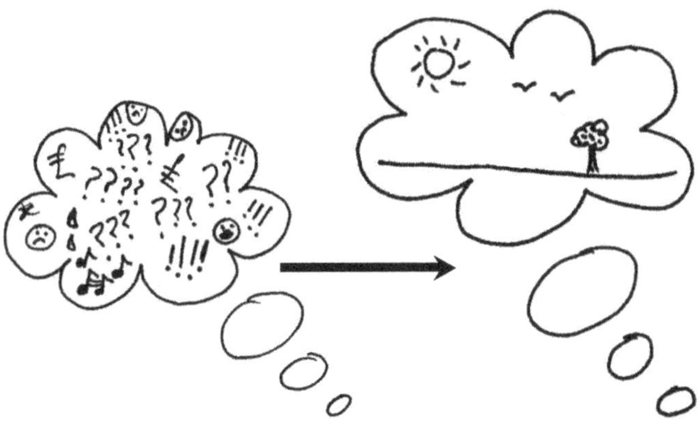

Aim

- To think about different places that you enjoy and take pleasure in being there, compared to places where you might not feel so comfortable.

Instructions

- **Introduction**: Find a place to sit in the room where you feel comfortable. Discuss what each person likes about their place. Find a place to sit in the room where you don't feel comfortable. Discuss this place. Remember you may need to refer to the group rules on safety and looking after each other during this activity.
- **Developing**: Think of somewhere you felt comfortable recently – describe, draw or write about it. What did you like about the place? Do the same for somewhere you felt uncomfortable.
- **Experienced**: Imagine a comfortable place, what would be there? Who would be there? What would you do? What would an uncomfortable place be like? What would the places smell, taste, feel or sound like?

Talking point

- Managing feelings.

Equipment

- Paper and pens for drawing and writing

Relaxation

Progressive muscle relaxation

Imagine your body as a map. Try to focus on each area of your body map and tense and relax each area so that you become relaxed.

Aim

- Identify the difference between tension and relaxation.

  OR

- Visualisation (not to be done if there are young people who may be psychotic).

Instructions

- Get into a comfortable position with your head supported against the wall.
- Tense and relax each muscle group twice.

Talking points related to this session

- Not knowing is ok.
  - If there are things you want to find out, plan how you will do this.

Session 17 Culture

Mindfulness

Cultural objects

Aim

- To experience and practise being in the moment, focusing on the here and now.

Instructions

- Do 3 minutes of mindfulness, rest or reflect, and repeat 3 minutes of mindfulness.
- **Intro**: Have lots of objects in a box with a hole in it. Taking turns, the young people put their hand in the box and feel an object, describe it to the group and guess what it is. Then they take it out and have a look.

Choose one object from a small group and focus on this.

- **Developing**: Select an object and focus on this.
- **Experienced**: Ask each young person to select an object. Discuss after the first 3 minutes which object they selected and whether they will try the activity with this object again or choose a new one.
- Remember to ask the young people the week before to bring in cultural objects if appropriate.

Equipment

- Range of culture objects that are suitable to be handled by participants

Identity

Festivals from around the world

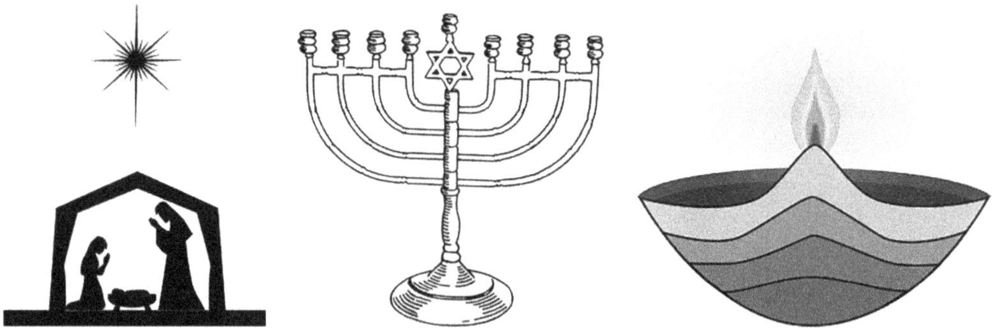

Aims

- To find out about different festivals from around the world and festivals the group have attended. To learn about the people that may go to these festivals.

Instructions

- **All**: Look at pictures of different festivals. Discuss who recognises each.
- **Intro**: Tell the group what you know about the festival or your memories. Take turns to listen to each other. Keep it brief.
- **Developing**: Each person chooses a festival they know, or thinks of one they have attended. In pairs, write/draw items associated with the festival. Young people tell other group members what they have drawn or written about.
- **Experienced**: Discuss the festivals each person has attended and add extras to the list by either writing or drawing.
- Include events that are seen by children and young people as part of their family culture including their faith.

Note: Young people could be invited to bring things from their own culture.

Talking point

- Everyone is different and that's ok – learn to love yourself.

Equipment

- Pictures
- Paper
- Coloured pens/pencils
- Art materials

Self-esteem

Family/School Events

I feel good when. . .

Aim

- To think about a family or school event that I have enjoyed and have been good at. I may also think about events that I haven't enjoyed as much and I may be able to think about why this is.

Instructions

- **All**: Discuss celebrations in our families and school, taking turns to offer one idea for each place. Complete 'Things that make me feel good . . . sheet (Session 4). Photos of families, school events etc. can be used to facilitate discussion.
- **Intro**:
    - Facilitator shares a cultural event with the group. Discuss what they each like about it. Would they like to be there? Why?

      OR
    - Young people act out a well-known cultural event, e.g. a birthday or the event that has just been described.
- **Developing**: Each describe a cultural event. What happened at the event? What was enjoyable about it?
- **Experienced**:
    - Each go around and describe a cultural event that they were involved in. What happened at the event? Did you enjoy it or not? What could you do differently to make it better? What could your family do to make it better this time? What did you enjoy about it? Would you do it again? Why?
    - What I think may not be the whole story – get other people's stories, get ideas from them to get a fuller picture.

Equipment

- Photos, pictures of events

Relaxation

Count down

Aim

- To tense body and relax 'in celebration'.

Instructions

- **All**: Count down from 10 to 1 and cheer as loud as possible – stamping feet can also be added for this. Then relax. Repeat this a few times. Facilitators will need to model this and really stamp and shout, which can be a bit embarrassing but the young people are more likely to relax and feel less self-conscious if facilitators do, so just go for it. Then the young people will get the idea that they are 'allowed' to do this and that is what is meant! It may take them a few times to get the idea of shouting as loud as they can.

Note: it may be worth informing anyone in the surrounding rooms that you will be doing this, so they are not alarmed!

If this is not felt appropriate, the young people can choose a relaxation activity from a previous week. Other celebration chants can be used if appropriate for the culture of those in the group or the setting.

Activity sheets for session 17

Thing that makes me feel good	What is it like? Why is it so nice?

Session 18 My future

Mindfulness

Choose an activity the young people have enjoyed – they may want to choose their own different activities.

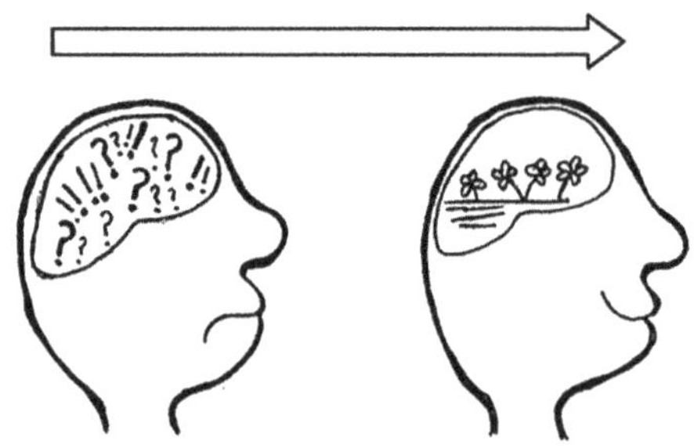

Aim

- To experience and practise being in the moment, focusing on the here and now.

Instructions

- Ensure you are clear who is choosing the activity and that you have all equipment needed for any choices you are offering.

Identity

Timeline and hopes for the future

Aims

- To think about what you want to be doing in the future.
- To think about what qualities you want to have in the future.

Instructions

- This is linked to the timeline created in 'My body – growing and changing' (Session 12). It is also linked to qualities or characteristics focused on in Session 14 ('Qualities and characteristics' worksheet).
- **Intro**: What do you want to do in the future? Short term – next week: I want to be in a play, go to a party etc. Or longer term: when I grow up I want to be a police officer. Draw these on the paper bodies.
- **Developing** and **Experienced**: Write or draw on your timeline what you want to do in the future. Aim to include three or four items within an appropriate time sequence, e.g. doing nurse training and then working as a nurse. This could include college, university, jobs, family life, friends, where you want to live etc.
    - What kind of a person do I want to be (qualities and characteristics)? This can be linked to the roles for inspiration, e.g. you need to be caring to be a nurse.
- **Experienced**:
    - Further discussion about how you can be these characteristics and what makes someone kind, mean etc. What does that mean for you? Are you some of these things now? What do you do now that is kind, mean etc.?

      OR

    - Write 10 things in answer to the statement 'I have discovered that I am . . .' and then share these with the group.

Self-esteem

Achievements

Aim

- Describe something that I am proud of and think about the skills I have.

Instructions

- Invite the young people to tell a real story about a time when they have done something they are proud of. Other young people and facilitators listening write down, draw or choose a card for the characteristics that they are showing through this memory/story.
- **Intro**: An adult tells the first story. The young people go around and say what they liked about it. They are encouraged and prompted to tell a story about something they have been proud of. Facilitators can think of ideas before prompting them.
- **Developing** and **Experienced**:
    - Young people tell a more detailed story about a time when they have done something they are proud of. Identify skills the young people have demonstrated through their story.
    - Everyone listening to the story writes down things they are good at/skills they have demonstrated in the story. When the story is finished, give feedback. Each person tells the storyteller what they thought or wrote down about the things they liked or skills. The notes can be given to the person to stick on their paper bodies.

Relaxation

My future relaxation activity

Aim

- To identify and record a preferred relaxation activity for future use.

Instructions

- Ask each young person to think of one relaxation activity that they would like to use in the future. Encourage them to describe or show the activity to the group.
- **Intro**: Record the relaxation activity the young person prefers. If they do not choose one themselves, give three choices that the facilitator has observed the young person to enjoy.
- **Developing**: Encourage the young person to record the activity themselves.
- **Experienced**:
    - Ask the young person to record their preferred relaxation activity and discuss where and when it may be useful for them to use.
    - As a group, all try your preferred relaxation activity.

Equipment

- Ensure you have paper, pencils, camera or photocopying facilities to enable each child to leave the group with a picture, drawing or some writing to remind them of their 'liked' relaxation activity.

Talking points related to this session

- Like vs. good at: You can like something that you are not necessarily great at.
- Working towards your own life goals.

Activity sheets for session 18

My future – I want to be. . .

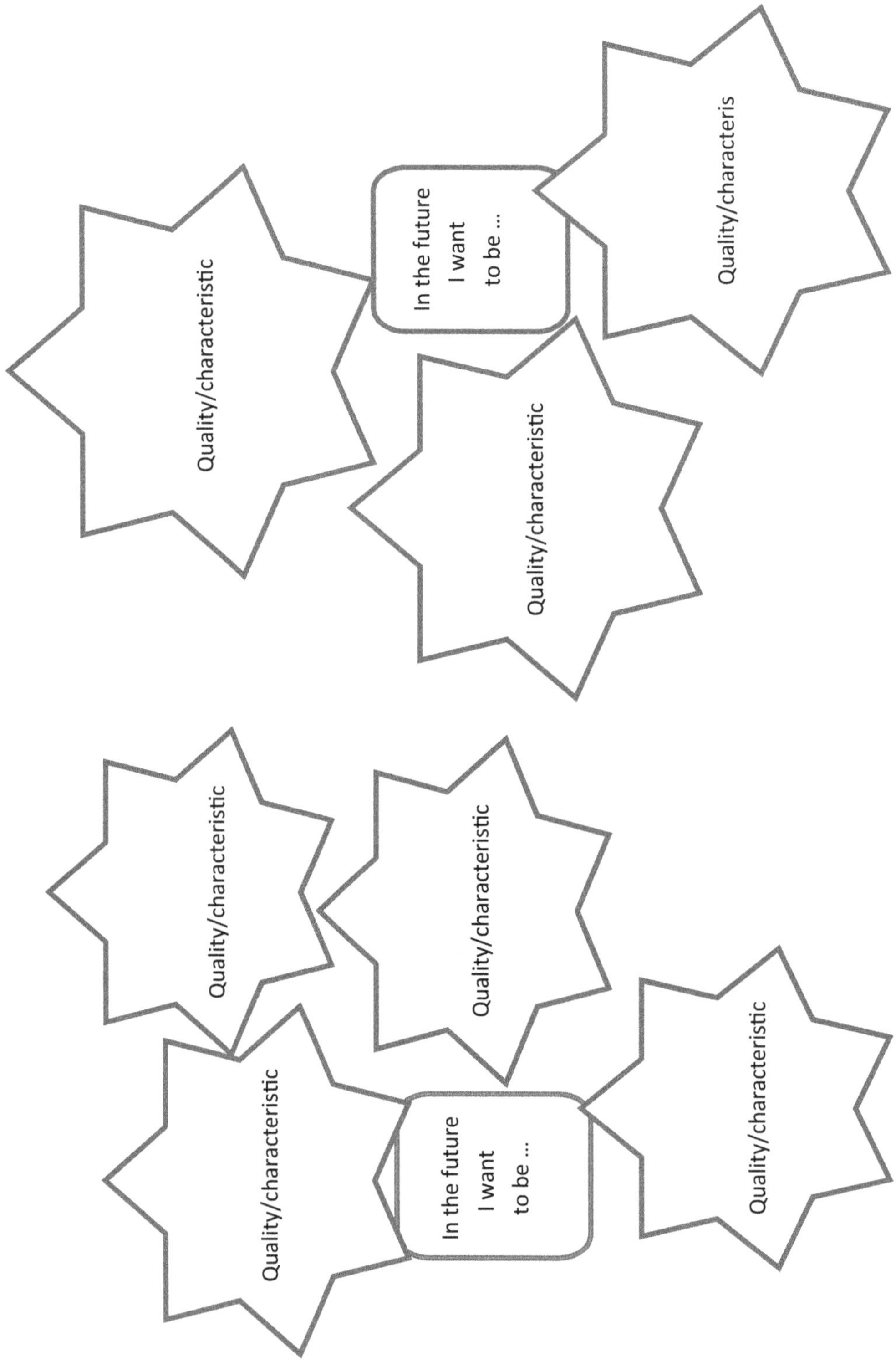

Session 19 My perfect place – summary and evaluation session 1

Mindfulness

Group choice

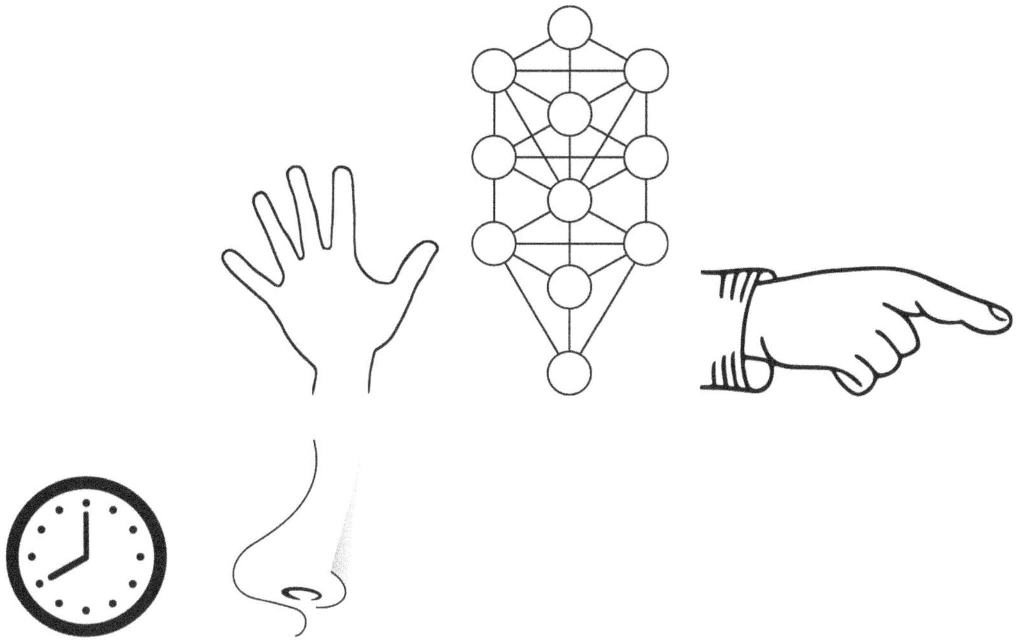

Look at your hand Colouring Watching a clock Smelling or Touching

Aim

- Identify which mindfulness activity that you have enjoyed the most and practise being in the moment.

Instructions

- **All**: Young people choose their favourite mindful activities and record on the sheet. The different objects can be laid out to remind them which they prefer.
- Try to extend the time of mindfulness by 1 minute (remember, 5 minutes is an aim depending on the group). You can try to stretch the young people as the group allows.

Discussions

- **Intro**: Go around the group and say one thing you noticed while doing this. What did you like?
- **Developing**: Go around the group and describe your experience.
- **Experienced**: Ask the young people to describe their experience and what makes this the favourite mindfulness activity.

Equipment

- Clock
- Colouring sheets
- Colouring pencils
- Fabric
- Textured balls and other sensory equipment
- Oils or other smells

Identity

Describing a memory

Aims

- Think about an imaginary or real place that would make you feel good.
- Think about what you would do in your favourite place.
- Who would be in your favourite place?

Instructions

- **Intro**: Think of your favourite holiday or outing with school, friends or family etc. Where did you go? What did you do? Draw these things and stick them on your paper body.
- **Developing**:
  - Go round the group describing your favourite trip/holiday/outing. Prompt them if they are having difficulty with the details, e.g. Who were you with? Where did you go? How did you get there? Where did you sleep/stay? Describe the landscape, e.g. sea side, hills forest, town (specific buildings), ice skating etc. What did you do? What did you eat?
  - Draw this and attach to paper bodies.
- **Experienced**:
  - Go round and say where your favourite holidays/outings have been. Who with? What did you do?
  - Think about what makes these so special for you. What are the common things that make you feel good (e.g. the people there, the activities, the types of places etc.)?
  - Imagine the most perfect place that you could be in. This could be imaginary or real.
  - Draw or write about these and put in folder.

Equipment

- Coloured pens/pencils
- Paper

Self-esteem

Creating your perfect place

Aims

- Use your work from all of the groups, i.e. your body outline or folder, to remember what you like and what you're good at.
- Create your perfect place where you are happy and relaxed.

Instructions

- **All**: Use your work from all of the groups, i.e. your body outline or folder, to remember what you like and what you're good at. Think about them, as they can be used for inspiration to create your perfect place and add the things you like, are good at and make you feel good from the work you have done over the all the groups. Therefore, summarising the groups into one piece. This can then be used to help summarise yourself in the 'event'.
- **Intro**: Pick one of the places you have drawn/thought about. What makes you feel good about this place/activity or people there? Draw or write or act or someone else can write/draw for you.
- **Developing**: Act out what you might do in your favourite place. You could invite other people in the group to play different characters in you drama, or you could draw your favourite place.
- **Experienced**:
    - Write a short story or poem about your favourite place. Draw a picture of this place. You could include what makes you feel so good in this place.
    - Encourage young people to think about the different senses, e.g. What can you smell? What can you feel (grass or sand etc., warm/cold)? What can you see? How does it make you feel (e.g. happy, calm, and comfortable)? Using the senses can heighten the imagination and be useful to help all young people explore this further and in more detail.
    - Look at your body/folder of work you've completed. There are lots of things on it. This is all the work that you have done over the group. This is a picture of you and it makes up some of your identity.

Equipment

- Coloured pens
- Paper
- Glue
- Folders
- Camera and a way to give young people a recording

Relaxation 1

My future relaxation activity

Aims

- Use the work that you have done in the session to help you think back to that time and relax.
- Have the courage to do something different from others. The young people may be doing different things from each other.

Note: There may not be enough time for the last relaxation session. The self-esteem activity above may be focused on as a completion of the groups.

Instructions

- **Intro:** Choose a picture of something you like to do to relax. Act out or describe.
- **Developing:** Use your picture and look at this. Imagine being there. Think about what you are doing. Imagine how you would feel being there.
- **Experienced:** Read your story/poem or look at your picture of your imaginary place. Imagine being there. Imagine the things that you see, hear, feel, smell, taste etc. Use these to help you feel relaxed as if you were in this place.
- Stick these to your bodies to finish them off. Take them home to show family or display them.

Equipment

- Different pictures of things that are relaxing, e.g. bath, playing with friends, stroking a pet, hug, talking to someone you trust
- Pictures of different relaxing scenes, e.g. beach, forest, stream, sunset, waterfall etc.
- Paper and coloured pens/pencils etc.
- Glue

Relaxation 2

Choosing a relaxation activity

Aim

- To choose relaxation activity together as a group.

Instructions

- Recall relaxation activities you have done [**Introductory** – with pictures, labels or drawings as a reminder; **Developing** and **Experienced** – try to recall as a group]. Discuss who liked which activity [**Introductory** – choose a picture, label etc.; **Developing** –also discuss what was liked and not liked; **Experienced** – include discussion of why people liked different things].
- Can you all choose to do the same one? Will you choose a few and do them all?
- Practise a relaxation activity.
- Discuss how choosing an activity went and how the relaxation was.
- Activities may include any from previous weeks or young people's own ideas. See Chapter 2 for summary of types of activities.
- Progressive muscle relaxation – Breathing – Sensory focus – Autogenic.

Equipment

- Comfortable chair or floor mats
- Equipment for the activities from previous weeks

Activity sheets for session 19

Mindfulness and relaxation activities I like

Mindfulness/relaxation activity	When are these helpful?	How were they helpful or not?

Session 20 Preparing for the event – summary and evaluation session 2

Mindfulness

Individual choice

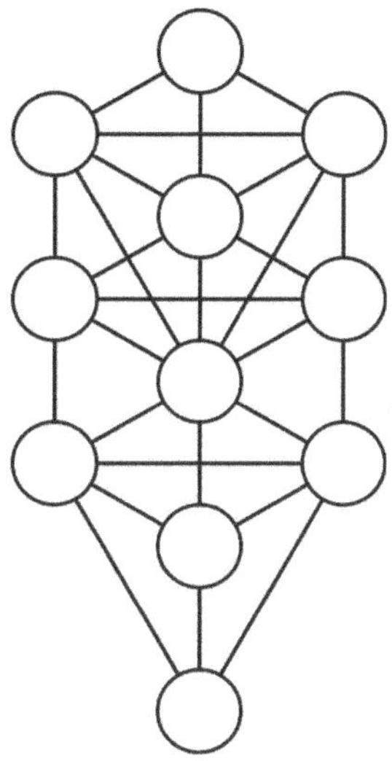

Look at your hand Colouring Watch clock Smelling or Touching

Aim

- Identify which mindfulness activity that you have enjoyed the most and practise being in the moment.

Instructions

- Try to do this fairly quickly, as the main focus this week is on preparing for and having the event.
- **All**: Young people choose their favourite mindful activity. The different objects can be laid out to remind them which they prefer.
- Try to extend time of mindfulness by 1 minute (remember, 5 minutes is an aim depending on the group). You can try to stretch the young people as the group allows.

- **Discussions**:
  - **Intro**: Go around the group and say one thing you noticed while doing this. What did you like?
  - **Developing**: Go around the group and describe your experience.
  - **Experienced**: Ask the young people to describe their experience and what makes this their favourite mindfulness activity.
  - **All**: If you have tried mindfulness during the week, what did you do? When? Why? How did it go?

Equipment

- Clock
- Colouring sheets
- Colouring pencils
- Fabric
- Textured balls and other sensory equipment
- Oils or other smells

Identity

I am discovering who I am!

And

Who I want to be

Aims

- Summarise all the work about who you are.
- Make a description of yourself using the work from the all the sessions from your body outline or folder.

Instructions

- All: Practise describing themselves using their bodies/folders and the work they have done over the groups at a level appropriate to their skills. They could practise by themselves, e.g. making a list of things they will say. Then practise in pairs to each other and then share with the group going around so everyone will share.
- **Experienced option**:
    - An option is after each person has shared, the group could give feedback. This could include what you liked about it and one thing that could be better or that they could do to improve.

    - Have a conversation beforehand about constructive criticism – what it is and experiences of this in the past – which will be helpful in preparing for it. This could include: What is constructive criticism? Is it easy or difficult to take on and learn from? Share any stories of times when constructive criticism has been useful in improving yourself.

    - Have the young people practise using constructive criticism to improve themselves. Enable the group to support and encourage others.

- **Optional extra**: Depending on the time, the experienced young people could use the 'Who am I?' 'What are my skills and qualities?' and 'What am I like?' worksheets, which may already have been completed in Session 14 and add a discussion of who I want to be. Young people can add 'Who I want to be' ideas to these worksheets. Go around and share after this. It is likely that the young people will need some 1:1 support to complete these.

Equipment

- Coloured pens/pencils
- Paper
- Body outlines
- 'Who I want to be' worksheet

Self-esteem

I can present my work at the 'event' – preparation

Aim

- To enable young people to share their understanding of 'who I am' with other people.

Instructions

- Each young person chooses a way of presenting their work at the event. *See chapter 'X on how to use the resource' for more information about the 'event' and ideas*. Ideas include. . . . See the section on 'Running the groups' for more details.

- **Make a DVD**: Describe yourself using the work that you have done over the group. Young people could use and show their paper bodies or folders whilst doing this. Have the young people practise this prior to filming. This can then be used in different ways depending on how you want to finish the group. Ideally, a recording could be copied and given to the young people. The work the young people have done over the sessions could be shared in different ways depending on your preferences and what is possible within the remit of your service.

- **Sharing in the last session**: All young people share their work and/or show their films to the group. Other staff or parents could be invited, if this is practical. If you are sharing work in the last session to each other, this is likely to take the whole session, as they may want to practise first.

- **Have a screening/event**: The young people could be invited to share their work with others. This could be at a small screening/assembly etc. Staff, friends and/or families could be invited, depending on how big an 'event' you want to make this. It could be something simple like reading out or showing and describing their favourite piece of work in assembly or simply at the end of the last group (this could take the place of the relaxation part of the group).

- **Display artwork**: A display and opening could be created with the young people's artwork. The opening could include screening of films and an introduction to the project. Or it could simply be a display where the group happened to show others the work. The young people could be involved with arranging and displaying their work and choosing the pieces they want displayed etc.

Note: It is important to get consent for recording etc. so follow your local policies.

Equipment

- Coloured pens
- Paper
- Glue
- Folders
- Camera and a way to give young people a recording

Relaxation

Favourite group activity

Aims

- Use the work that you have done in the session to help you think back to a time where you have felt relaxed.
- Imagine your perfect place and relax.
- Practise a relaxation activity that you have found helpful.

Note: There may not be enough time for the last relaxation session. The self-esteem activity above may be focused on as a completion of the groups.

Instructions

- **Intro:** Choose a picture of something you like to do to relax. Act out or describe what you would do there. This could be a game where others guess what you are doing and where you are.
- **Developing:** Use your picture and look at this. Imagine being there. Think about what you are doing. Imagine how you would feel being there.
- **Experienced:** Read your story/poem or look at your picture of your imaginary place. Imagine being there. Imagine the things that you see, hear, feel, smell, taste etc. Use these to help you feel relaxed as if you were in this place.

Equipment

- Different pictures of things that are relaxing, e.g. bath, playing with friends, stroking a pet, hug, talking to someone you trust
- Pictures of different relaxing scenes, e.g. beach, forest, stream, sunset, waterfall etc.
- Paper and coloured pens/pencils etc.
- Glue

Talking points related to this session

- Managing feelings.
    - Feeling nervous about sharing their work at the event.

- It is natural that young people may be feeling nervous about sharing their work. However, this is a golden opportunity to address these worries and work through them, helping them overcome fears of doing something challenging and achieving something. Each young person will have something unique that they are worried about. It may be helpful to encourage them to informally talk about this during the preparation for sharing their work. There is some more explanation about this in the session plan.

Appendix A
Description of the four elements

Mindfulness is about being in the moment, thinking about what you see, hear, feel, taste or smell *now*.

It helps you think less about other people worries, or the future.

Be in the moment

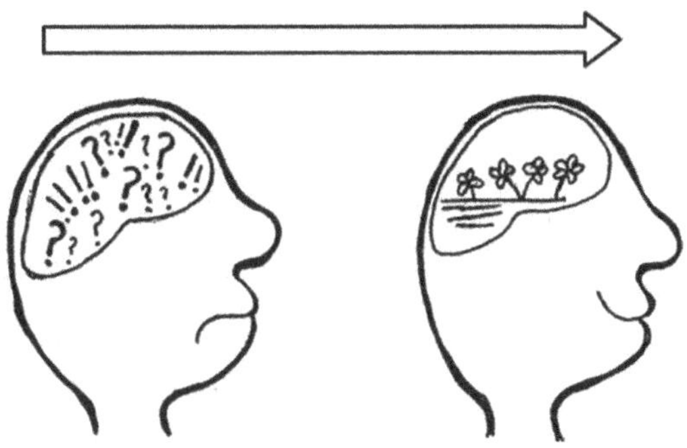

Some people use mindfulness activities to feel calm and settled.

Self-esteem is about valuing yourself – What skills do you have? What are you good at? How do you feel and think about yourself in a positive way?

What is good about you?
What skills, characteristics do you like about yourself?

Identity is about who you are and who you want to be – who are you?

What are the important things about you? How are you different from other people? How are you the same as other people? Are you part of any groups?

Relaxation – relaxing your body and mind, learning to feel peaceful

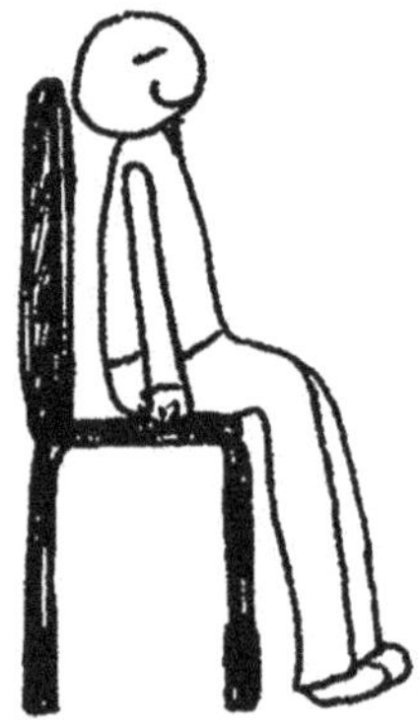

Appendix B

MISER symbols and session plan

Date – Topic -	Activities	Facilitator leading
Mindfulness 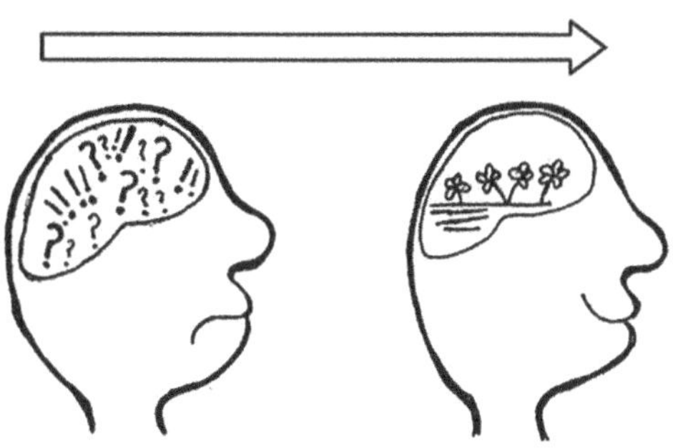		
Identity 		

Self-esteem 		
Relaxation 		

Appendix C
The topics list

Either use as a list or cut them up for young people to choose topics to use in an activity.

Introduction

My body – what do I look like?

Colour

Senses: sound, vibration and smell

Food – what do I like?

Food from around the world

Clothes – what do I like?

Clothes from around the world

Everyday life – what do I like?

Sport – what do I like? My teams and games

Exercise – my body and relaxation

My body – growing and changing

Gender – my body and stereotypes

Relationships and my family

Nature

Places

Culture

My Future

My perfect place – summary and evaluation 1

Preparing for the event – summary and evaluation 2

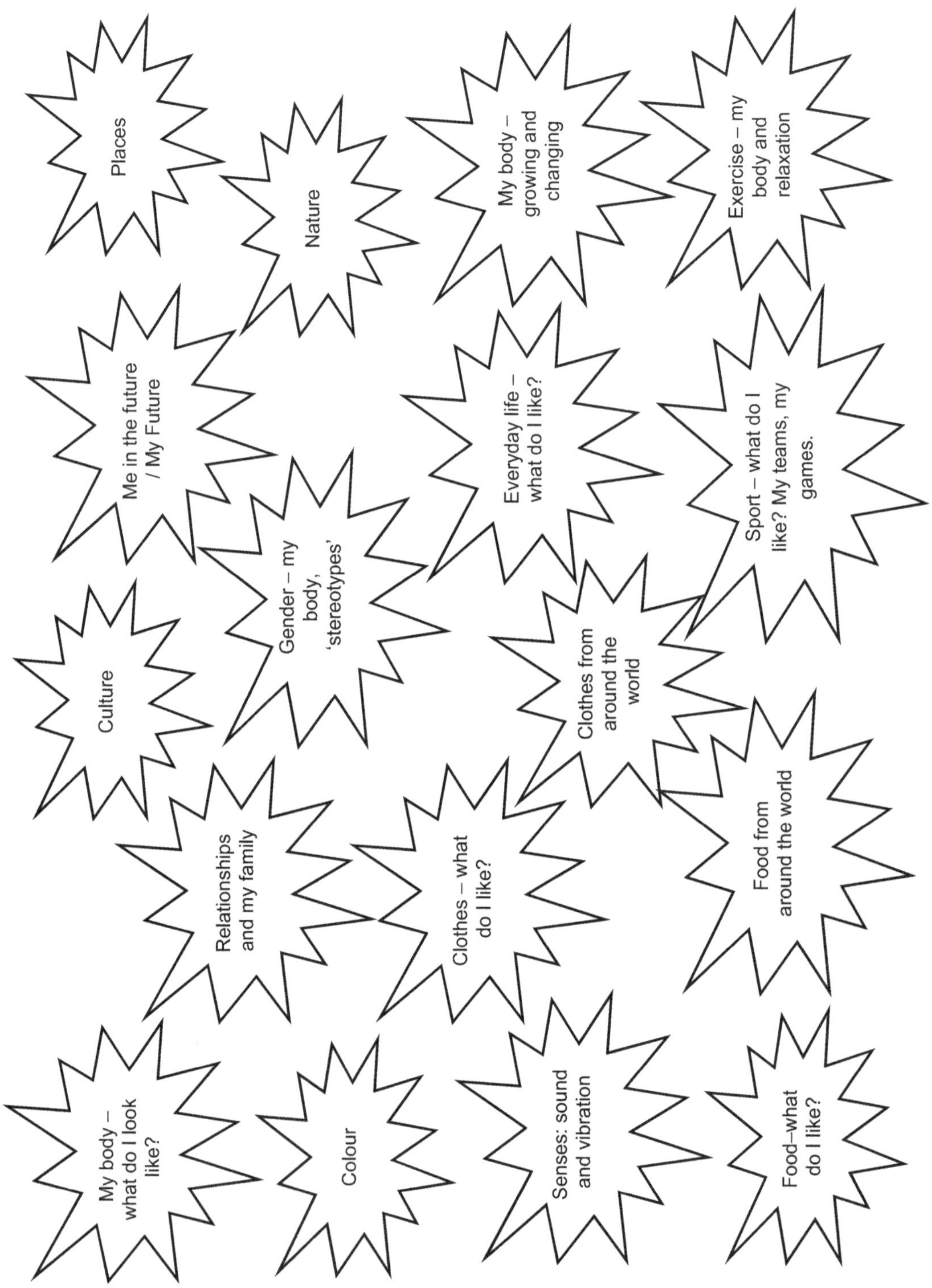

Appendix D

Group outline plan and evaluation form

Discovering who I am – group planning and evaluation sheet			
Session topics	**Core activities to include**	**How did it go? (include young people and facilitator perspective)**	**Who was there? Young people and facilitators**
DATE **TOPIC**	M – I – SE – R –		
DATE **TOPIC**	M – I – SE – R –		
DATE **TOPIC**	M – I – SE – R –		

DATE TOPIC	M – I – SE – R –		
Staff final evaluation of the group			

Appendix E
Talking points

Either use as a list or cut them up for young people to choose talking points to use in an activity

Mindfulness

Identity

Self-esteem

Relaxation

We aren't all good at everything

Managing difficulties in life

Not knowing is ok

Promote healthy lifestyles

Different people have different needs

Our actions and language have an impact on others

Making mistakes and trying again

Persevering

Getting along with others

Coping with difficulties

Everyone is different and that's ok – learn to love yourself

Like vs. good at: You can like something that you are not necessarily great at

Managing feelings

Assertive, compared with passive and aggressive

Working towards your own life goals

What I think may not be the whole story

Appendix F

'Discovering who I am' and my goals

Name: Date:

My Goal 1	1	2	3	4	5	6
	7	8	9	10	11	Review date:

My Goal 2	1	2	3	4	5	6
	7	8	9	10	11	Review date:

Appendix G

My goals examples and template

My goals

Name:________________________________ Date:__________

Things I find difficult and I want to be better at:

- I get angry all the time. I want to stop being angry and be more relaxed.
- I can't ask for help. I get embarrassed and worry what people will say or think of me. I don't want people looking at me.
- I get really nervous about talking in front of others. But I really want to be part of the assembly.

My Goal	Rating	What can I do to achieve my goal?	What happened? How did it go?	What happened? How did it go?	I'm getting better! (Rating)
By the end of the group I will have tried different relaxations and chosen my favourite	3 – I'm not very good at relaxing	Try the different relaxation activities every week.	I did not like the muscle one.	I like relaxing with music.	6
When I start to feel angry I will ask for time out. I want adults to help me make the situation better by talking.	1	Notice when I start to feel angry. Listen to adults when they ask how I'm feeling and answer. Ask for time out when angry. Talk about the situation after.	I got angry threw my work. I cried. I spoke to adults and felt better.	I felt angry when Jane ignored me. I wanted to hit them. I asked for time out. Adults helped me talk to Jane and it was difficult.	5
I will ask for help once in a group when someone asks me if I don't understand.	2	Be brave. Put my hand up. Tell myself "I can do it". Ask an adult when others are busy.	Ahmed (staff) asked if I had a question I said no but I didn't understand.	Ahmed (staff) asked if I had a question and I asked a question. It was hard. But no one else was watching.	✓ 3
By the end of the groups I will explain my work in assembly.	5	Complete work in groups. Practise what I'm going to say. Breath.	I did it! I was really nervous before but Beatrice (staff) helped me and I did it!	–	7 ✓

Rate 0–10 (0 = never, 5 = half the time, 10 = all the time)

My goals

Name:________________________________ Date:__________

Things I find difficult and I want to be better at:

-
-
-
-

My Goal	Rating	What can I do to achieve my goal?	What happened? How did it go?	What happened? How did it go?	I'm getting better! (Rating)

Rate 0–10 (0 = never, 5 = half the time, 10 = all the time)

My goals

Name:______________________________ Date:__________

My Goal	Steps	What happened?

Appendix H

Consent letter: a template of a letter to parents and carers

Dear Parent/Carer,

We are running a therapeutic group called 'Discovering who I am' and would like to invite your child to attend this group.

The aims of the group are:

- Discovering and managing my emotions
- Discovering and developing what I can do
- Discovering and developing myself with others
- Discovering who I am

See the leaflet attached for more information about the benefits of the group and talk to your child about these before the group starts.

The group uses a variety of different types of activities to support the development of the young people. Sometimes we use video to look back at how things have gone and think about how we could do things differently. Food is used within the group. At times there may be things like photos or objects that would be useful to bring from home. Please only bring things that you are happy for your child to share with others.

The group will run every week on (date) __________ at (time) ____________ for (duration) ____ Place___________. The group facilitators will be _______________.

Consent form

I/we give our consent/do not consent for ______________ to attend 'Discovering who I am' group.

I/we would/would not be happy for my/our child to be videoed in the group for use in the group.

Please list below (or on a separate sheet of paper) any allergies, medical conditions, anything to improve access or other information that would have an impact on your child participating in the group.

We would like to share with you how your child is getting on in the group. Please let us know the best way to contact you.

Email:

Phone:

We would be happy to discuss any questions you have about the group.

Yours Truly,

Group facilitator Group facilitator

Appendix I

'Discovering who I am' leaflet

'Discovering who I am' is a group for young people who are struggling with self-esteem, believing in themselves, having hope and confidence, having difficulty getting things done and getting along with others. Through being in a small group of young people that may have different struggles, it is hoped that the group will feel safe and be able to trust each other. The group is confidential, which means that no one should talk about what other young people have done or said in the group to anyone else. The aims of the group are:

Discovering and managing my emotions

- Knowing my emotions.
- Using mindfulness and relaxation activities to feel calmer.
- Coping with my emotions.

Discovering and developing what I can do

- To create, work towards and achieve my goals.
- To try new things, possibly make mistakes, and then succeed.
- To do more myself and complete work.
- Be playful and have fun, which will help me cope with difficult things.

Discovering and developing myself with others

- Build good relationships.
- Be accepted as I am.
- Learn to accept others with their faults.

- Practise getting on with others.
- Seeing things from someone else's point of view.

Discovering who I am

- To decide who I want to be and explore how I can achieve this.
- To grow in self-esteem and confidence.
- To help me cope with difficulties.
- To learn and practise decision-making, being creative and using my imagination so I find things that I enjoy (or not enjoy) and therefore discover more of who I am.

Mindfulness activities

Mindfulness helps you to stay focused and concentrate on school or work. It can help people to deal with anger and other emotions that distract them from being happy. Sometimes other skills become easier when we are mindful. When we're doing mindfulness, we are trying to focus on what is happening in our bodies or around us at that moment. Focusing on the here and now, not the past or future. It's not easy – it is a skill like all others that sometimes needs time to be practised and experienced to understand it. So it may seem like a waste of time at first, but carry on with it. There is much research that shows it's helpful for both young people and adults.

The group will start with a mindfulness activity, which will be repeated with a chance to share in between. It may start with just a few moments but will increase throughout the weeks as young people get used to this.

Identity activities

Identity is who you are as an individual. The things that make you special and who you are. It includes your appearance and personal characteristics, things you're good at, likes, dislikes etc. They are also the things that make a group of people different from others, e.g. supporters of a particular sports team. Having a strong sense of identity helps people understand who they are and helps develop self-esteem. It helps people be flexible and achieve the best they can. It develops as we grow up and lots of things influence this, such as family, friends, school, teachers, community, race, religion, hearing or deaf etc.

The groups start with the young people creating an outline of their bodies. Each week the work from the group will be added to these, either directly on the bodies or on worksheets cut out and stuck on to help create a picture of themselves.

Self-esteem activities

Self-esteem is the confidence in who you are and what you can do. It grows and develops throughout life. Having a stronger sense of self-esteem means people feel happier, make and keep friends, and will try harder when faced with challenges. They will be more likely to take care of themselves physically and emotionally and less likely to be a victim of bullying. It also helps in managing life's up and downs when difficult things happen.

Young people are invited to actively complete activities to gain a sense of achievement and belief that they can do things and are worthwhile.

Relaxation activities

If relaxation is the opposite of being tense, then we need to understand this. We are tense when we are highly aroused, e.g. angry, anxious, worried, stressed etc. Our muscles become tense and our breath quickens, we may have more worries etc. So being relaxed means having fewer worries and it means slowing our bodies down, including breathing and letting go of the tension in our muscles and bodies.

These activities are designed to give young people the opportunity to experience different types of relaxation activities and to try them out in a safe environment.